B Coolid
Coolidge, Rita
Delta lady : a memoir

$25.99
ocn918590683
First edition.

Delta Lady

Delta Lady

A MEMOIR

RITA COOLIDGE

with MICHAEL WALKER

HARPER

An Imprint of HarperCollins*Publishers*

HarperCollins books may be purchased for educational, business, or sales promotional use. For information, please e-mail the Special Markets Department at SPsales@harpercollins.com.

FIRST EDITION

Designed by Paula Russell Szafranski

Library of Congress Cataloging-in-Publication Data has been applied for.

ISBN: 978-0-06-237204-8

16 17 18 19 20 OV/RRD 10 9 8 7 6 5 4 3 2 1

For Priscilla Coolidge
I will love you forevermore,
for all reasons, foreverlasting

Contents

Delta Lady

Prologue

was doing the dishes when I realized I was going to be all right. It was March 1977 and my life was in turmoil. I was about to turn thirty-two and my tumultuous six-year marriage to Kris Kristofferson—the love of my life and father of our three-year-old daughter, Casey—was nearing an acrimonious end. Two months earlier, I'd miscarried our second child, whom Kris and I had both hoped, unannounced to the other, would heal our relationship. I had been numb to the world ever since. But that afternoon, washing the dishes in the simple ranch house that I'd found for us in the hills above Malibu—where I had once thought Kris and I might live for the rest of our lives—I suddenly heard my voice float out of the kitchen radio.

By then I was used to hearing myself on the air. I'd sung on everything from Stephen Stills's "Love the One

You're With" to Eric Clapton's "After Midnight" and Ray Charles's R&B classic "Busted." I'd released four solo albums, which tended toward rock-tinged pop and romantic ballads. Kris and I had won a Grammy in 1974 for our performance of Kris's "From the Bottle to the Bottom" and another in 1976 for "Lover Please." (Our signature number on stage was "Help Me Make It Through the Night," which when things between us were right we sang as much to each other as to the audience.) My albums had sold moderately well and I was thrilled to have devoted fans, but I'd yet to break through as a solo artist.

I'd just released my sixth album, *Anytime . . . Anywhere.* My producers David Anderle and Booker T. Jones and I had decided to record several covers of R&B hits, including Jackie Wilson's "(Your Love Keeps Lifting Me) Higher and Higher" built around a really inventive arrangement by Booker that just floored me and my label, A&M, which released the song as the first single off the album. "Higher" has such an affirming vibe, and I was looking for hope wherever I could find it that afternoon in Malibu when the song came on the radio. I shut off the water, wiped my hands on my apron, and listened. "Your love," I sang a cappella, at a hymn's tempo, "is lifting me higher . . . than I've ever been lifted before . . ." After a full stop, a bass drum thumped four times, a killer guitar riff kicked in, and my version of "Higher" took off like one of the gulls kiting over Los Flores Beach far below.

Listening to myself sing about the redemptive power of love stirred my heart for the first time in months, and in that moment I had an epiphany: Not only would I survive this difficult time, but I would thrive. As I have heard so many times from other artists whose ships finally came in, it was also such a typical moment. The song that would become my anthem—which I close my shows with to this day—arrived while I was laid low by grief and, literally, washing the dishes.

The next thing I knew, "Higher" had shot straight up the charts to number 2. I'd never had a song remotely that big. *Anytime . . . Anywhere* hit number 6 and was certified platinum, selling more than a million copies. I'd never sought stardom or success at that level but it had come anyway, at the bleakest moment of my life. It also put me on equal footing, professionally, with Kris. We toured together behind *Anytime . . . Anywhere* but it was different from past shows. He would be on stage for his portion of the show and people would be yelling "Rita!" between his songs, and I'd feel so bad about that. Despite our differences, Kris was proud of my success, even though it might have been tinged with envy—he was in great shape with his movie career (he'd costarred with Barbra Streisand in *A Star is Born* the year before) but more than anything wanted to be recognized as a singer and songwriter. He'd written classics like "Me and Bobby McGee," Janis Joplin's biggest hit, and "Sunday Morning Coming Down," for Johnny Cash, and had cofounded, with Willie Nelson, Waylon Jennings, and other renegade singer-songwriters, the so-called Outlaw movement that had shaken Nashville's traditional country music scene to its foundations. But as his movie career took off, Kris spent less and less time on his music, which frustrated him and fueled some of the heavy drinking and anger that inevitably was turned toward me.

Touring together when we were having such grave problems in our marriage was a challenge. For years, I'd been pressing Kris to go to counseling with me, but he steadfastly refused. We both had strong personalities and tended not to back down in an argument. When you factored in Kris's drinking—though he'd abruptly quit after *A Star Is Born*—and his desire to fulfill his outlaw image whenever and wherever possible, we were rapidly approaching an emotional cul-de-sac that I knew we might not escape. The worst part of it was dealing with his womanizing. Connie Nelson—Willie Nelson's former wife and still one of my best friends— used to laugh and say, "Isn't it great? We're the younger women." Guys usually left their wives for younger women, and Kris was nine years older than me. Little did Connie and I know (but we should have): there's always a younger one.

It wasn't that Kris's fame blinded me to his faults. Before Kris I'd had serious relationships with Leon Russell and Graham Nash, and had spent plenty of time around famous—and famously unpredictable—

musicians such as Joe Cocker and Eric Clapton. But by the time of *Anytime . . . Anywhere* Kris had escalated his emotional attacks. He didn't think I was as good a writer as he was—I wasn't—and had begun to actively belittle my work. I tried to keep the marriage together—not only for Casey's sake, but because the love that had enveloped Kris and me was unprecedented in both of our lives and, I believed, worth fighting to keep.

Kris and I were on the road—Casey was with us—when the breaking point arrived. I had returned to our hotel suite from running an errand and Kris just started yelling at me, needling me, demanding to know where I'd been. It was a fight we'd had a hundred times before. Casey was pleading, "Please stop, please stop." I turned to Kris and said, "Done. I'm done. I can't do it anymore." That's when I made the decision to leave. But the actual walking out the door came later that year when Kris was shooting Michael Cimino's *Heaven's Gate* in Montana, and I sussed out that he had something going on with his leading lady, Isabelle Huppert. At that point, after all we'd been through, I just didn't feel like I fit in to his life anymore—unless I was willing to be the wife who stays at home and turns a blind eye.

I don't remember confronting Kris on the *Heaven's Gate* shoot. I don't remember the words that were said, though I must have said them. What I do remember is walking out of the hotel suite and going home finding a house in Hollywood to rent packing everything up and taking Casey with me. It didn't hit Kris until he walked in the Malibu house and saw that some of the furniture was gone. Of course once I left, Kris was willing to do all the things I had asked him to do for years. He wanted to see a marriage counselor, but it was too late. "Once I walk out the door, I don't come back," I had always warned him. "Once it's done, it's done." And now it really was done for me.

Kris and I were together eight years. Eight years. There were fabulous times. We literally made beautiful music together. What we went through—from the moment we met and for eternity—is something bigger than I've ever had with anybody else. I never laughed with anybody in my life like with Kris. Everything we did was larger than life. When it was good I was absolutely over-the-moon happy. And when it was sad it was almost too much to bear.

The success of *Anytime . . . Anywhere* was a gift that propelled my career and my life for years afterward. I'll always be grateful for the doors it opened for me. But I feel like when that all happened I was so young, I didn't really know my craft. I think there is something to be said for the years of living the music that you've been singing, when you understand what the song truly means. When I recorded "I'd Rather Leave While I'm In Love," I thought, That's the silliest thing I've ever heard—who would do that? And then I walked through that door myself three months later.

Life needs art to express emotions we find too painful or unknowable to express ourselves. To paraphrase Apple's slogan, whatever you're going through, there's a song for that. As my Cherokee grandmother told me when I was a girl in Tennessee, "It's all about listening."

CHAPTER 1

Growing Up

'm told when I was a baby I could sing before I could talk. I do remember singing harmony with my sisters in church—my father was a Baptist minister—when I was two. I could barely say the words but I could sing. I was the shyest little kid in the world unless somebody said, "Would you sing?" Mother and Daddy and my aunts and grandmothers and my sisters, Priscilla and Linda, all sang, so music was a natural part of our lives, just like sleeping and eating. Singing with my sisters gave me a sense of harmony and how important that is. So we grew up realizing the value of music and art in the lives of children from the time they were born. It also marked us as outsiders—I think deep down inside I probably always knew that. Mother would say, "Honey, we're not like other people." And Priscilla and I, all of our lives, we've told our kids: We are a family of artists and singers, and things function differently in our lives, and we see things and hear things differently.

I had the best parents in the world. They just adored each other. They never argued. The only time Mother ever got mad at Daddy was when he took his boat out and a storm was coming in and she had to send the Coast Guard to find him. That was the only time I ever heard her raise her voice to him, and they were married seventy-five years. Daddy was Cherokee and Mother was of Cherokee-Scottish lineage, which was common in Kentucky and northern Tennessee, where I was raised. Because Kentucky was so much like Scotland a lot of Scots settled there. And because the Scots and Cherokee were both tribal—the Scots had clans and so did the Cherokee—there were a lot of Cherokee-Scotttish intermarriages. Well, that and the fact that the Cherokee women were so incredibly beautiful. Daddy never felt anything but a great deal of pride in his Cherokee blood, despite being spat upon when he was a child in Texas. Mother was a teacher. She didn't get paid for it but always stayed after and made sure that the school she taught in had a music program. She did it on her own time because she knew how important music was for kids—you've got to have more than ABCs and math. It's not a full program of learning and relating to the world without music and art. Daddy did the same thing with his Sunday school students—everything about him was creative. He was a visual artist and his paintings are all over my house today.

I really was Scout from *To Kill a Mockingbird*. I related to that little girl and to the racism that Atticus Finch refused to be a part of and how he stood behind and with the black people, because that's what Daddy did. I was that little girl going to white churches with my family in Lafayette, Tennessee, a small town northeast of Nashville just south of the Kentucky border. I never saw a black person until I was six years old, when Mother and I were in Nashville. Black people were not even allowed to drive a truck through Lafayette, or for that matter, all of Macon County. Supposedly, during the Civil War, a black woman had killed a white baby and they had hung her in the holler behind my grandmother's house. I knew the tree where it was said they had hung her.

Later, when we lived in Nashville, a black woman—her name was Miss Maggie—would come and clean our house. Mother would let me go and spend the night at her house and go to church with her because in our house, the color of your skin didn't matter; it only mattered if people were disrespected or treated badly because of that. And then Daddy would be up in arms about it because of what he'd been through as a part Indian boy in Texas. That was just not anything that his kids were ever going to experience. When we played cowboys and Indians we'd say, "Bring 'em on, we'll kick your butts."

The one thing I learned from watching Daddy from the time I was little is that if there's some kind of injustice being done or spoken about and you don't say something, then you become a part of it. So it became so important to me to do that, to let my daddy's voice live in me and behave that way wherever I went. When I was in grade school I couldn't allow people to say bad things about people of color in my presence—Daddy wouldn't tolerate it, so neither would I. I would say, "I can't stand here and be with you if you're going to speak this way." You move away from prejudice because it will stick to you if you don't. I think Daddy was as close to God as any human being. He taught by example; he really walked his talk and lived what he preached in every way. We didn't sit down for Thanksgiving or Christmas dinner until he knew that everybody who didn't have what we had—any of the church members or anybody in the county that he knew needed something—had been taken care of; he just would not be able to sit down.

There was a little girl who came to our school, Rachel. You could always tell the really poor kids when they would migrate through—her family had homesteaded this old house a few miles down the road from us and Rachel actually walked to school. It was probably five miles. Everybody was so mean to her. And I just couldn't take it, so I became Rachel's best friend. One day I decided to go home with her after school and when I got to her house and opened the refrigerator there was nothing. I was going to call my parents and tell them where I was, not realizing that Rachel didn't have a phone. Meantime, I'd given Rachel my coat—it was gray wool with a burgundy velvet collar and cuffs—because they had no heat in her house. I thought, Well, I'll give Rachel my coat and I'll get another one. I was walking down the road with Rachel when Daddy came along looking for me and he took her home. Afterward I'm sure he made certain something was done for that family. But I didn't get a new coat—I got a hand-me-down.

My parents met when they enrolled in Madison College, a Seventh-day Adventist college in Nashville, in the thirties. They both worked their way through school because it was the Depression and neither of their families could afford to send them, and they both were intrepid and fearless. After Daddy graduated high school he hopped a freight train and rode his way from Texas to Nashville because he had heard about Madison and wanted to be a doctor. He got there with just the clothes on his back. After Daddy married Mother, they moved to Lafayette, her hometown. He was of course swarthy because of his Cherokee blood, and when he came to town they said, "Charlotte's married a gypsy." I think they would rather have not had someone that they considered of color in their little white town. But Daddy not only stayed, he won everybody's hearts. He was a man who in many ways had survived just by making things work. In the forties he opened a restaurant on the town square and built a Laundromat and figured out how to build a big drum dryer. He could do anything he set his mind to, it seemed. He could build a house, do all the plumbing, even hang the drywall with a little help from me and a T square. He had been a lineman for the county when I was a child, so he knew how bring in electricity, too. Without going to seminary, he won Pastor of the Year in California after he and mother moved there in the 1970s. And his faith was insurmountable. There would be times in the church or in our family when we would need something and Daddy would say, "Don't worry, it'll be okay, it'll come through." And it always did. There was never a mountain that he couldn't climb.

But for such a restless, accomplished man he was equally grounded—he always found time for a moment of repose where he could reflect on his life or simply unwind. When I was in high school Daddy and I would get up at four in the morning and put the boat in the St. John's River and fish for a couple of hours. I loved to fish with him—just sitting on the boat and the water so still and peaceful, maybe catch a red snapper or two before class. Afterward I would change in the car and he'd drop me off at school. But if the fish were biting he'd say, "You don't need to go today, do you?" and we'd spend the rest of the day on the river. (For Mother and Daddy's sixtieth anniversary, I took them halibut fishing in Alaska.)

My maternal grandmother, Mama Stewart, was born in 1878 and lived above the holler in Lafayette for most of her adult life. She grew up on a farm in Kentucky;

when her mother passed and her father remarried and the kids didn't like the woman that he married, they cut out the woman's head in the family portrait and replaced it with their mother's picture—it's one of those hysterical photos every family seems to have, and it hangs in my house today. Mama Stewart's husband, Papa Stewart, was a circuit-riding, banjo-and-fiddle-playing preacher. He would go around to farming communities because people lived on these huge farms and there weren't enough people to have a local church. So he would come and spend the weekend; they would have a barn dance on Saturday night and then he would preach on Sunday morning. He was apparently a very dashing man. When he came through my grandmother's town they had the barn dance on Saturday night and she had on a red dress and had let down her long black hair. When he met her that night he decided on the spot that she was the girl that he was going to marry. He came back a month later and asked her father if he could court her. He took her for a buggy ride—she told me he tried to kiss her and she wouldn't let him. After they married he wouldn't go near her for more than a month because he wanted to make his point that he could play hard to get, too—he made her go to him. Papa Stewart was ten years older than her; I think she was fifteen when they married.

The first family picture of Mama and Papa Stewart was taken outside their tiny cabin. There are three little kids—one girl is holding a cat—and they're just out in the dirt. At some point they moved from Kentucky to just across the border to Tennessee. They are both buried in Kentucky, in Scottsville. The Cherokee society wasn't migratory—they lived in permanent villages across the South, from Kentucky to as far west as Mississippi. Mama Stewart had an aunt, a full-blooded Cherokee, who had survived the Trail of Tears, the terrible forced march of the Cherokee and other Southern tribes to the Oklahoma territory in the 1830s. (To comfort themselves as thousands died along the trail, the Cherokee sang "Amazing Grace"—the hymn's English lyrics had been translated into Cherokee by the missionary Samuel Worcester, and when sung in Cherokee it is considered their national anthem. I sing the Cherokee version in my concerts today, and it never fails to bring an audience to rapt silence.) Mama Stewart would talk about her Cherokee people and also about the Scots because she was a direct descendant of Mary, Queen of Scots. But she didn't speak any Cherokee; for the most part, especially in the South, flaunting one's Indian blood was not rewarded. (My paternal grandmother, Mama Coolidge, could "pass" and didn't broadcast the fact that she was Cherokee—she always said she was Castilian Spanish.)

The Cherokee people were matrilineal—women had a revered role in the Cherokee society. We had women chiefs. When a couple married, the man would live with the woman's clan as opposed to the woman going to the man's. Women were not really considered to be adults and fully in their power until they were fifty-five. That's why the grandmothers were always held in a place of great reverence in our family. We did everything for our grandmothers, and we got so much back from them.

Because Mama Coolidge lived in faraway Ventura, California, we didn't see her so much growing up. (After I'd moved to Los Angeles when I was twenty-two and was breaking in as a background singer, I drove up to see her. I knocked on the door, saying, "Mama Coolidge?" I found her outside, sitting in a tree, composing a poem.) Mama Coolidge—she always wore red petticoats under her skirts—opened my eyes when I was little. She once took Priscilla and Linda and my brother, Dick, and me out in the woods in the middle of winter and said, "Find something that you think is ugly. God doesn't make anything ugly, but find something you *think* is ugly." We found all these gnarly burrs, things that had shriveled, and put them in our baskets. And we took them back to the house and Mama Coolidge brought out ribbons and paints and started weaving together all the things we'd gathered that we thought were ugly, and she made these beautiful baskets. It taught me to be able to see the beauty in everything.

I think that because Mama Stewart was such a nurturing human being, my mom was, too. For Mama Stewart, it was always about listening: listening to the birds, listening to the music, listening to the words. What are the melodies that make you feel good and what are the ones that don't make you feel good? What are the sounds that scare you? It's all about listening.

My older sister, Priscilla, was my best friend. She always told me that before I came along she was waiting for me. When my other sister, Linda, was born, Prissy took one look at her and said, "No—that's not her." Priscilla used to tell me that when I arrived two years later, "I said, 'She's here.'" When we were little it was always me and Priscilla, sneaking out of our room at night to go and lie under the stars. She would say, "That's where we came from." She had a great imagination. She also had this incredibly huge, powerful, all-over-the-place singing voice. My voice was simple—I could depend on it and knew what I could do and what I couldn't do. Priscilla could do anything. And did. After I'd graduated from Florida State University and moved to Memphis, we had a sister act—she wore a gold lamé dress and I had a silver lamé dress and we sang Bee Gees songs. We didn't make much money but at least we were singing.

From the time she was little Priscilla expected that she would be a star—she just naturally had the persona of a celebrity. Hollywood talent scouts came through Lafayette one time and heard her sing—she was this little bitty thing with this great big voice—and they wanted to take her. They told my parents that she could be a big star. And I'm sure she would have been, but Mother and Daddy said absolutely not. Priscilla was very open and free in the way she thought and the way she dressed and who she was. She was like my sympathetic twin. As we grew older, our lives seemed to parallel—we'd buy the same clothes without knowing it. You could walk into Priscilla's house or my house and you wouldn't know if it was mine or hers. We were so much alike and yet so different—I cry at the drop of a hat, but not Prissy. She was three and a half years older than me and bigger than life— very outgoing and flamboyant; she never walked out the door without all her makeup on and dressed to the nines, whereas I'm much quieter and subtler. As her younger sister, I was always kind of in her shadow, admiring her and what she accomplished but knowing I wasn't going to be like her. Having my friendship with Priscilla, along with two parents who loved each other more than life itself, and such creative and nurturing grandmothers, gave me a good, solid foundation for when I later entered the world of rock and roll. I pretty much knew who I was.

When I was in seventh grade—we were living outside Nashville by then—one day at school they announced, "We have a new student." And what do you know, but it was Little Miss Dynamite herself, Brenda Lee! She'd just had a huge hit song, "One Step at a Time," and all of a sudden Brenda was in my school—wow, she's just like we are, she's normal. Except she's tiny, like four foot nine. The cutest little thing you ever did see. Brenda and I became really good friends and we were on the cheerleading squad together. People called us Mutt and Jeff because she was so little and I was almost as tall as I am now. We used to sit at the piano all afternoon and sing "Great Balls of Fire," trading lines—"You shake my nerves and you rattle my brain . . ." Brenda spent more time at our home than she did at hers because at that time she was living in an Airstream trailer with her mother and her little sister—her father had died three years before and she was the family breadwinner. Not long after moving to Nashville she released her biggest hit, "I'm Sorry," and toured England, where four unknowns from Liverpool were her opening act, which has got to be the greatest piece of personal trivia to whip out at a party: "Oh, by the way, the Beatles opened for me." Brenda and I remain friends and toured Europe together in 1985 with Tammy Wynette and our old hero, Jerry Lee Lewis. It was one of Tammy's last tours. I loved her so much; she sang with such a teardrop in her voice. During the tour, my band and Jerry Lee's broke off and played some gigs in Switzerland. I was walking into the hotel when Jerry Lee and his latest wife came ambling through the lobby wearing these loooong fur coats, I mean fur coats to the floor. Jerry Lee came up and said, "Rita, I want you to meet my new wife." And he turned to her and said, "This is . . . uh . . . uh . . ." And his wife answered, without missing a beat, "Number six." Jerry Lee, of course, was a piece of work. They would actually carry him to the stage and he would have a bottle of Jack Daniels at his lips— glug, glug, glug. Then he'd play the show, tear it up, and have to be carried off.

By the time I was thirteen, I lived what seemed like an ideal life: I didn't have to worry about anything. My life was getting up on Sunday morning and going to church with Daddy, going to school and making really good grades.

And suddenly something happened to me that upended my entire world.

We were driving down Dickerson Road outside Nashville on our way to the market when this car came across the median at about sixty miles an hour and hit us head-on. I was thrown through the windshield, Daddy had a concussion and was out cold, and both of Mother's legs were fractured. I was lying in front of the car. Blood was streaming out of my head from a severed artery. Mother managed to get out of the car and started screaming for help. And out of nowhere, this man came walking out of the woods. He had dark brown hair, an average-looking man. He reached into the car and got a piece of cloth and pressed it against my head to stanch the bleeding. After the ambulance came to take me to the hospital, Mother looked around to thank the man but he'd disappeared. We put ads in the paper: "Does anybody know who this man was? He saved our daughter's life." We never found out. There was speculation he was an escaped prisoner—he was wearing striped pants—but there were no prisons anywhere near the crash. He was like my personal Boo Radley—or guardian angel.

At the hospital there was a doctor that Daddy knew, a plastic surgeon named Dr. Rydelle. My face was severely cut from the windshield glass—one of my eyebrows was completely detached and hanging by a thread. The next night I was supposed to have my first car double date, so I kept saying, "Somebody just put a Band-Aid on it, it'll be fine, just take me home, I have a date tomorrow night." This doctor probably spent six hours stitching my face back up. He literally gave me a face. I was out of school for six weeks. I was such a mess—my whole face was black and blue—that when they brought me home my grandmother took one look at me and started sobbing. Even Mother would walk into the room and start crying. For days it was like that. I finally said, "You know, y'all really can't keep doing this." My favorite teacher, Mr. Milton, used to come by every day after school and bring me my homework and sit with me. And every day he would say, "You're look-ing so much better." He was that positive reinforce-ment I needed. By then Priscilla was on a Grace Moore Scholarship at the University of Tennessee studying opera, even though she was only sixteen—that should give you an idea of just how smart and ambitious she was. I already missed her terribly, and when I took my first car trip two months after the accident, it was to see her. The stitches were out but my face was still pretty gnarly. Priscilla was out front when we got there, waiting. And when I got out of the car and ran into her arms she just looked at me and said, "Well, I don't see anything wrong—you're gonna be the next Miss America." She was always, always like that.

Still, sixty stitches in your face when you're thirteen years old is not an easy thing to overcome. Until I learned to drive, I couldn't ride sitting up in a car because I thought every oncoming car was going to hit us. So I had to lie down in the back. (When I started dating, I would have to tell the guy, "Okay, I have this problem because I was in this accident. I can't look out the windshield, so I have to ride with my head down.") When I went back to school, I went to a friend's house for a slumber party. And I found this note that one friend had written to another. It said, "Rita is a teenage Frankenstein." And it broke my heart. But it also challenged me to be everything, to do everything. I just decided: This is not going to take me down—this is going to make me stronger

The accident was a jolt of reality, my first really big slap in the face. Things were not ever the same for me again. You can't really recover completely from something like that because you carry the physical and emotional scars with you always, like you do with any great upheaval or calamity in your life. When I saw *Patriot Games*, the Harrison Ford thriller, there's a scene where Anne Archer has a head-on car collision. I didn't know it was coming—I screamed and started crying and had to leave the theater. And that was over thirty years after the accident. I had no idea that was still so much a part of me. But, really, everything that you live—good, bad, and otherwise—becomes a part of you.

I often reflect on choices—the ones we consciously make, but especially the ones that happenstance or fate, depending on your outlook, make for us. When we moved to Florida when I was a sophomore in high school—Daddy had gotten a new ministry there—I had to say good-bye to all my Tennessee friends, including my first true love, Gordon Gregory. They say never trust a guy with two first names, right? (I later discovered there might be something to that particular piece of folklore after I became involved with the drummer Jim Gordon in Los Angeles.) But Gordon Gregory was a good guy. He had pearly white teeth—he actually became a dentist—and was just adorable. He was a football player, I was a cheerleader. If I'd stayed in Nashville, who knows? We might have gotten married right out of high school. Things could have gone quite differently. It's like the great Tom T. Hall song, "Pamela Brown," where he lists everything he would have missed—the " lights of cities," the "foreign countries," and "all of my good times and all my roamin' around"—had he married Pamela Brown, the "well-intentioned good girl in our town." I must have already known that, deep down, I wanted to be more like the hero of Tom T. Hall's song than a Pamela Brown.

You do what you have to do. That's just it, that's the bottom line. It's amazing what we can do and what we can survive and what we can get through. Not only that, but to be able to look at it like, Well, if that hadn't happened to me I wouldn't know this, or, I wouldn't be this person. It's the blessings, those hidden blessings that carry you through when the most horrible things seem to be happening. I didn't really understand that after the accident, but I do now. Even when I was taking care of my dying mother and it was the hardest thing I'd ever done, I knew that I was in a sacred space and that there were blessings all around me.

Because in the middle of every pile of shit there is a pony.

CHAPTER 2

Memphis

Even though I knew I was different than other people, I spent a lot of my life trying to prove that I could be like other people if I chose. After we moved to Nashville, I remember starting at Maplewood High School and everybody saying, because of my dark complexion, "She must be Cuban." So I decided: Well, you know what? I think this little Cuban is going to be your head cheerleader next year. When I enrolled at Florida State in 1963, I thought: Let's see if I can be in a sorority. And I pledged Alpha Gamma, just to see if I could do that, too. After being a cheerleader and the mascot of the Y Club and all that, it was a natural progression, I suppose, even though I only did it for the challenge. So I joined, along with my friend Stuart—Mary Stuart Simpson—who pledged with me. But before long the rituals and unreality of it all began to really get on our nerves. I did learn a few things. I learned that when you set the table, the knife

blade has to be turned in because during "the waw-wa"—
that would be the Civil War—it could've been considered
a weapon if the blade was turned out. There was also a
lot of talk about "What did your great-granddaddy do in
the waw-wa?" They talked about the Civil War and what
their families did and which battles they fought and how
their families had bought the property where the battle
of so-and-so was fought and had preserved the parts of
the fort that were still standing. They were all puffed up
with pride about that and it just amazed me. They were
still living in the Civil War. And you know where that
puts people of color.

I was a straight A student before I went to college.
Once I got to Florida State and realized the freedom that
a Baptist preacher's daughter had on weekends, I was no
longer a straight A student. I came close to flunking out.
The dean of women happened to be a friend of Mother's
and called me in one day and told me I was going to have
to get down to business. So I did make Dean's List from
then on. And it didn't take long before I realized that,
in fact, I didn't want to fit in badly enough to belong to
a sorority. Stuart and I were pretty well dug in to the
university's art department, where the campus misfits
seemed to gravitate, and were rapidly becoming rebel
hippies. We had moved into the bohemia part of our lives
and were making sure we got the signifiers right. Stuart
kept saying hippies can't have kinky hair—she had red
hair that was just like Little Orphan Annie's—so we'd

iron her hair until it looked reasonably enough like Joan Baez's. Needless to say, none of this was going down well at the Alpha Gamma house.

What finally tore it for us was that the elder sisters used a minor infraction of the house rules to make an example out of our roommate. The house had a ludicrously early curfew, and if you missed it, which everyone did, you could usually count on one of the sisters to let you in the back door so you'd never get in trouble. Somehow our roommate got caught trying to sneak in one night and they singled her out for a lot of self-righteous ridicule and suspended her. The hypocrisy enraged Stuart and me. So one night before a chapter meeting we drank just enough beer and went up the back way without the secret knock and said, "Fuck y'all," tossed our pins on the table, and left. (Stuart and I found out later that our roommate went back to the sorority anyway after we had thrown it all in for her.) Weirdly, when I played the Florida State homecoming ten years after I graduated, I drove down sorority row and there was a huge WELCOME BACK, RITA! banner hanging from the Alpha Gamma house. I thought to myself, Really? Y'all don't remember what happened? Apparently, my pin had been turned in to one of the alums in Tallahassee who liked me and never sent it to the national chapter, so I was still a member in good standing. (This same woman showed up at one of my concerts later and handed me an envelope—inside was my pin.) So Stuart got booted but I never did.

After I left the sorority house and got my own apartment, I did nothing but sit at night and listen to Robert Johnson and Muddy Waters and Mississippi John Hurt. The street I lived on had a lot of little houses rented to students from the art department, and they were all listening to those records. Nobody else was doing that. Everybody else was listening to the Righteous Brothers and whatever was on the radio. I started getting into Bob Dylan. And he became a very major influence on me. I started parading around campus not in my cute little madras skirts and Weejuns, which everybody wore, but in overalls that had paint all over them from whatever I'd done that day in the art department. I let the paint build up until I was a walking Pollock, the intended effect being: Wow, she must be really good, look at all that paint on her overalls. That and to show I wasn't a conformist. All of us in the art department did that—we wore our outsider status with pride. We also always had a lot of weed, which we'd decided was vital to the creative process, thanks to this guy who came through Tallahassee every year, like Johnny Appleseed, to plant pot and would tell a couple of people on campus—in the art department, of course—where it was planted.

We were also acutely aware of the civil rights movement. There were then maybe thirteen black people out of ten thousand students at Florida State—Florida A&M in Tallahassee was the unofficial black university.

I couldn't wait to go to their football games because their halftime show with the marching band was over the moon. My art department friends and I would carry signs and march in front of the businesses off campus that would not allow black students to come in and sit down. We had eggs and tomatoes thrown at us and God knows what else. But you know what? It blended in just fine on those paint-splattered overalls. I didn't feel like I was one of the freedom riders or the brave people in Mississippi who were in physical danger—nobody was getting killed in Tallahassee. But I did feel like I was doing what I had to do because of the way I had been brought up. And Stuart was right there with me. We were using our voices as opposed to just sitting by and being silent and not expressing an opinion about the change that had to come. Prejudice was so entrenched in the Deep South at the time, even in my own extended family. I would go up to Tennessee to see my aunt Phynis, who had a dress store—the Style Shop—and moonshine liquor in the back. After the shop closed for the day, she'd bring out the moonshine and we'd have a swig or two and smoke a cigarette. One night, during the height of the civil rights movement, Phynis was sitting there, swinging that leg and smoking the cigarette, and said, "Well, honey, we gotta get home tonight because you know all the niggers on Nigger Hill's comin' down and we've heard they've got rifles and they're gonna start shootin' white people." And I said, "Phynis, what are you talking about?" She said, "That's out down the road there, where all the niggers live."

Unsurprisingly, I was opposed to the war in Vietnam—I had already lost friends who had been drafted and sent to fly airplanes and didn't make it home. One of my best friend's brothers went out in the woods and shot his toe off so he wouldn't be drafted. I didn't think it was cowardly. He wasn't a killer. He'd rather lose part of his foot here than lose his life fighting in a war that he strongly objected to. I felt that our voices should be heard. There were a lot of us and we had the power to change things. Bob Dylan was singing "for the times they are a-changin'." Music had become a social voice. I hope Bob Dylan realizes how profoundly he changed this country and the people of our generation. Because he—and we—surely did.

The summer after my freshman year the people from the 1964 World's Fair came down and recruited students to work at the fair in New York City. My best friend from high school, Mary Leah, and I decided that if our parents would let us go, we'd do it. We rented an apartment in Brooklyn with a couple of other girls. It was my first trip out of the South. I was nineteen. As an art student, I was thrilled because every day, before work—I sold tickets inside the World's Fair Pavilion, the big geodesic dome—I would get in line and see Michelangelo's *Pietà*.

And when I left work, I would go by and see it again. It was the most beautiful sculpture I'd seen in my life. I saw it twice a day all summer long, and that was the best part of the summer. My brother, Dick, had a friend who lived in New York named Sandy, who kind of looked out for me and would take me places. He took me to the Copa to see Bobby Darin, which of course was very cool. And then, it could have been the same night, he was taking me back to Brooklyn on the subway and these guys got on, pulled out blades, cut open the pockets of some man who'd passed out, and took his money. There was nobody else in the car. Sandy made a gesture like he was about to get up, and in a flash one of the guys zipped over, sat by me, and put the razor to my throat. He just held it there and stared at Sandy as if to say, *Don't fuck with me.* I was, of course, terrified. I didn't make a sound but tears were streaming down my cheeks. Sandy was trying to communicate with the guy: "Be cool, be cool." Then the train stopped and they got off. I'm sure I burst out sobbing as soon as they were gone. I told Sandy, "That's it, I don't want to live here anymore." He somehow talked me into staying.

I'd brought my guitar with me from Florida and, before the scare on the subway, I would go by myself to the Village into these clubs and sing folk songs. There was a place called the Basement—I'm sure it hasn't been there in decades—where, if you had a guitar, they'd let you play. It was very *Inside Llewyn Davis,* if you've seen the Coen brothers' movie about the folk scene in the early sixties. I'd started singing with some folk bands while I was at Florida State; I waitressed at the Hotel Duval restaurant and on the weekends we would play at the hotel's LeRoc Lounge. That was Rita, Rail, and Raker John; and then I joined another group with one of my professors—Dick Kraft, who was a brilliant songwriter and musician—called the Fourth Day Windfall. And, no, I never knew what the name meant, but it sounded folk-y. I also formed a rock band, R.C. and the Moonpies (the Moonpies were all members of the Sigma Chi fraternity) that played Sigma Chi houses in Florida and Alabama. So I'd had a little practice, plus of course I'd been singing and playing with Priscilla and Linda for years. I was actually well received in the Village that summer—they liked me, this little hippie Indian girl. But after the subway incident I was too traumatized to do that anymore. I pretty much stayed with the crowd and did my job at the World's Fair and couldn't wait to get home.

When I graduated Florida State in 1967, I moved to Memphis— Daddy had a church there by then—thinking that I might teach school because I had majored in art and minored in art history, English, and elementary education. Instead, I turned back to music. Because I could sight-read, I was able to get a job as a singer at this jingle factory, Pepper Tanner. I made a decent living singing the call letters for radio stations, among other things, and it led to my first record deal. Pepper Tanner had formed its own label, Pepper Records, and I recorded a song for them, "Turn Around and Love You," written by Donna Weiss, who later became a major songwriter and background singer in Los Angeles—she co-wrote "Bette Davis Eyes," and she and I sang together on Joe Cocker's Mad Dogs & Englishmen tour in 1970. For my promotional photo I wore my hair in bangs with a little flip and Mary Jane shoes and a blouse with a little white collar. They wanted to change my name to Antoinette Lovely. Seriously. And I told them, "Do you think my parents will recognize me if I'm Antoinette Lovely? I don't think so. I want my parents to be proud. I want to represent my family. I think Rita Coolidge is just a fine name." That was the end of Antoinette Lovely.

I was living with Priscilla, who was starting her own singing career in Memphis. Earlier, she'd run off and secretly married a student, Paul Satterfield, whom she met the summer after her freshman year at the University of Tennessee, and later had two children, Paul and Laura. She and her husband had since divorced and I moved in with her and helped take care of the children.

It wasn't long before I started making my way into the Memphis music scene, which at that moment rivaled Detroit's as the country's most influential for black music. And I started meeting some interesting people. One of them was Don Nix, who was a saxophone player with the Mar-Keys and a man-about-town. Don and I used to go out to the airport at night and pretend we were Sonny and Cher and that we'd just gotten off a plane—even though Don was as tall as a tree and Sonny definitely was not. I swear, people would come up and ask us for our autographs and we'd sign them. It was just something silly we did. After I moved to LA, Cher and I actually became good friends—she's so smart and such a great singer. Kris and I had sung on *The Sonny & Cher Show*, and one day, after she and Sonny split, she called me out of the blue and said that because of the nature of her relationship with Sonny, she realized that she had no friends of her own. She said to me, "Will you be my friend?" Cher and I did become really good friends, to the point that, bless her, she offered to sing background vocals on one of my albums. I was in the control room with David Anderle, my producer, while he recorded her with four other background singers. David said through the intercom, "Somebody out there's a little bit flat." And one of the girls turned to Cher and said, "I don't want to say any names, but Cher, don't quit your daytime job."

Through Don I got an insider's introduction to the Memphis music scene, which in the late 1960s was nearing its creative peak. Don was an incredibly prolific songwriter, producer, and arranger and was one of the architects of the Memphis sound on Stax-Volt and Hi Records. It was thrilling to be in the thick of a scene where classic hits from Al Green, Otis Redding, Wilson

Pickett, Ann Peebles, Isaac Hayes, Rufus Thomas, and Sam & Dave seemed to arrive weekly. Through Don I met many of the musicians and producers who would influence my career. Members of Don's band, the Mar-Keys, also recorded as Booker T. and the MG's and had a huge hit, "Green Onions," on Stax. (Booker would go on to play a crucial role in my music and in my life.) Though dominated by African American artists, the Memphis scene differed from the scene around Motown not only in the style of music—a more driving, Southern feel tinged with jazz and traditional rhythm and blues—but because the musicians, producers, and sometimes the bands were multiracial; two of the four members of the MG's, Steve Cropper and Donald "Duck" Dunn, were white. It was encouraging, although ironic, that a city in the heart of the segregationist South could nurture a scene where talent and the love of playing trumped race with such spectacular results. Then I met Teenie.

Mabon "Teenie" Hodges was already a legend in Memphis—an ace guitarist in the Hi Records rhythm section and a songwriter, too. He cowrote "Take Me to the River" and "Love and Happiness" with Al Green and became his main sideman and collaborator. Teenie got his start when Willie Mitchell, the producer and trumpet player who ran Hi, took him under his wing. Teenie told me that he met Willie when he was painting houses between gigs to make ends meet. He had actually been hired to paint Willie's house, and Willie came out to see how the job was going and told Teenie, "Well, you're doing a mighty fine job, young man." And Teenie said, "I can paint, but I can also play guitar." Willie said, "Well, you finish painting and then come in and show me what you can do." After he finished painting the house, Teenie went inside and broke out his guitar. Willie heard the unique sound that Teenie had and took him on the road with him and taught him everything he knew. That was the beauty of the Memphis music scene in those days—gatekeepers like Don and Willie weren't just open to considering unknown talents, they actively sought them out, which is how Teenie went pretty much overnight from painting houses to becoming Al Green's guitarist and shaping the sound of all those hits.

I can't remember exactly how I met Teenie—I'm sure it was at a recording session. But it was like he'd just always been there—one of those people. Teenie and I were best friends, we were lovers, we were absolutely crazy about each other. Teenie was married—according to him, he and his wife weren't together, but who knows? I'd never met anybody like Teenie. He was very soft-spoken and just so sweet and a beautiful, beautiful man. Really dark skin, a fabulous mop of hair. Teenie was a room rocker. He never had to say anything. He just walked into a room and his energy was so magnetic that people would suddenly be drawn to him. I would spend every minute that I could with Teenie. If he had time to come by in the afternoon, even just for a glass of tea, it made my day. He was pure sunshine.

Teenie took me places that other white people didn't get to go in the black community in Memphis. There was a club called the Rosewood—the official name was Bennett's Club Rosewood—a former movie theater at the corner of South Lauderdale Street and Rosewood Avenue. The Rosewood was where all the black Memphis soul greats hung out, drank, and woodshedded. When Teenie took me I was the only white girl there that night. Nobody seemed to care—maybe because I was an Indian, people accepted me—but I'm sure arriving with Teenie had a lot to do with it. That night Ike and Tina Turner were performing. Teenie and I went backstage to the dressing room and he introduced me to Tina—this was while she and Ike were still married. She had her wig on and was putting on her dress and doing her makeup. She and Ike were not having a good night, apparently. Then she said something about Ike splitting her head open. I wasn't sure I'd heard her right and asked, "What do you mean?" And Tina suddenly took off her wig and showed me this scar that ran from the front of her head all the way to the back. Tina had a really pretty speaking voice—soft, very feminine, a little seductive and raspy, but underneath just determined and strong. So she very matter-of-factly showed me this scar—and I know about scars, obviously—and then said to me just as matter-of-factly, in that voice of honeysuckle and steel, "This—this is what he does." Of course, I thought it was unusual that she would reveal something to me that was so awful and private, but she knew Teenie and trusted him and loved him like everybody else did, so if I was a friend of Teenie's I was therefore okay.

God, the places that Teenie would take me. We'd go over to Hi Records and if Al Green was recording he would make sure I could sit in the control room on the session. Through Teenie I had gotten to know Willie Mitchell and his wife and daughters and we used to play cards all night long over at Willie's house while the guys were in the studio. At the time I was living with Priscilla and she had a roommate who was very, very prejudiced and made several comments to me about Teenie to the effect that "if that Teenie comes over here again . . ." This is before Priscilla and I got our own house. I think it was probably this girl's comments that pushed us into finding our own place. To me Teenie was a beautiful man who just happened to be black.

Then Teenie and I introduced Priscilla to Booker T. Jones, the keyboardist and leader of the MG's. They fell in love and decided to get married. When word got around, the Klan burned a cross in the front yard of Mother and Daddy's house. Daddy was away on a revival but Mother was there alone. She called the police, terrified. It was appalling that the Klan could still pull these acts of cowardice and terrorism, in a city as big as Memphis, so blatantly. One night I was driving home from a session through Overton Park in my little green Volkswagen and got lost trying to get to the other side. And suddenly I came upon a Klan rally in the middle of the park. There was the bonfire, the guys in the white hats, the white robes. I managed to get the car turned around and get away without being seen. I've never been more frightened in my life—it was far more terrifying than having a knife held to my throat, because that was random and the rally was a premeditated act of pure hatred.

I was still in Memphis when Martin Luther King was assassinated. Priscilla and I had our own house by then, which we shared with Venise Starks, who was Otis Redding's girlfriend—Otis was married but they had a thing going on. Her bedroom was papered with eight-by-ten glossies of Otis. Venise's claim to fame was that every year she sang at Elvis's New Year's Eve party. She was also a fabulous dancer and had a fabulous little body. And I think that's why Elvis wanted her there, because she was the cutest thing in Memphis. She was always creating dances for people. One night the phone rang and when I answered this unmistakable voice said, "Hey, this is James. Venise there?" I went up to her room. "Venice—James Brown is on the phone." It turned out that James was coming through town and needed a new dance—the dance Venise created for him was the Popcorn.

After the assassination word spread pretty rapidly on the news. The directions were: wherever you are, get to your homes. It really was like being in a war zone because nobody knew what was going to happen. That night things started to get really bad. We lived on the border of a black area of town and a white area, so everything kind of spilled over. When shots started being fired and the curfews were imposed, we never walked by a window. For five days and nights, until the curfew was lifted, we crawled on the floor if we were in the front part of the house. There was just so much chaos and so much sadness and frustration and anger. And now being so connected to Teenie and Willie and his family, it became so much more of a real thing. To all of us, Martin Luther King was not just Martin Luther King—he really was the king. He stood for everything that so many of us wanted —for equality and dignity for people of all colors.

The Memphis scene was never quite the same after the assassination. Mother didn't want to live in the South anymore—to have to endure the terror of a cross burning in your front yard because your daughter was marrying a black man, and then have the greatest black leader of our times struck down from a motel balcony, was just too much. It wouldn't be long before Mother, Daddy, Priscilla and Booker, and I would leave Tennessee for a new beginning in California.

I'd noticed for a while that all Don Nix seemed to talk about were these husband-and-wife musicians Delaney and Bonnie Bramlett and their LA-based keyboard player, Leon Russell. Don talked about Leon like he was the greatest of all musicians, how he'd led the Shindogs, the house band on the TV show *Shindig!*, and played piano like Professor Longhair. So when Leon came to Memphis with Delaney & Bonnie—they were recording their first album for Stax Records—I felt as if I already knew him through Don. I just fell in love with Delaney & Bonnie and the whole vibe around that group, which was rooted in Southern rhythm and blues and rock and roll, a sound that was different from anything that I had heard other than on *Randy's Record Hi-Lights* on WLAC, the great Nashville clear-channel radio station that in the 1950s beamed R&B all the way into Canada on a good night. I hadn't heard white people singing like Delaney, Bonnie, and Leon—they never really got the credit for their influence. Years later, Elton John told me that he never would have done what he did and been where he was if it weren't for Delaney & Bonnie. They influenced a lot of people. And I was one of them.

As I got to know Leon I was fascinated by him and really liked him a lot and knew that, like me, he was different. Delaney and Bonnie were not like other people, either, but in a really wonderful, familiar way. Leon was not like other people in a strange way—he had long hair, and a really long beard, both prematurely gray, and piercing blue eyes. That in itself was enticing, and it was not very long before Leon and I were spending time together. (As for Teenie, he and I had always seen each other when he could manage—he was married, after all—and we had an unspoken understanding that as much as we adored each other, we weren't exclusive to each other.) Leon also loved the way I sang, as did Delaney and Bonnie, and the three of them kept saying I really should be singing out in Los Angeles. So when the sessions were over and Leon asked if I would drive him back to LA, I said yes. I'd been through so much in Memphis in so short a time—meeting Don and dear, dear Teenie; singing sessions; and recording my first single, which was starting to get regional airplay around the country. I'd made some forays to Nashville to audition for the record executives there, because although I loved the Memphis scene, the artists getting signed in Memphis tended to be black, whereas my background was more of a folk singer. The Nashville auditions were ridiculous, like inquisitions—they asked for my résumé before they'd listen to me sing. The labels rejected me flat out. They said I had no star quality and when they saw I had a teaching degree suggested that I should go back to Memphis and teach.

But I have always had some really great luck or whatever it is—synchronicity, being in the right place at the right time—when a door would open and opportunity would be there. So when Leon and Delaney and Bonnie said "Come sing with us," that was the affirmation that helped propel me to California. My face had long since healed from the accident—you needed to look really hard to see the scars—but those sixty stitches had severely challenged my self-confidence. My time in Memphis had allowed me to begin to rebuild it. Certainly, people were attracted to me because I was an anomaly: a Southern Cherokee belle. But I had a college education and was determined to live my dream—and I was doing pretty well. I felt my relationships were based more on depth than on beauty. I was coming into my power and realizing that I was able to do anything I aspired to do. And that gave me confidence to leave Memphis for LA with Leon. I took only my suitcase with some clothes. I was just going to test the waters, or so I thought.

Leon had bought this blue, '56 or '57 Thunderbird convertible—not the little two-seater with the fins but the four-seater—which we proceeded to drive across the country in November 1968, just before Thanksgiving. Leon never dealt with a single human being except me on the whole trip. I did all the checking of us into the motel after dark so they couldn't see who was in the car. Leon never got out of the car, especially in Texas. He was so paranoid about the way he looked—in the late 1960s, longhairs were still openly harassed outside of big cities—so I would say, "Yes, my husband is in the car but he's not feeling well, I'll check us in."

When we got to Los Angeles and the Skyhill Drive house where Leon lived he got out of the car and immediately went inside. I just assumed that I was expected to get the bags which, of course, I'd been doing along with everything else. So I got the bags out of the car and I walked up into this strange house. And as I was walking down the hall, I passed this person I'd never seen before. And I said, "Hi, I'm Rita." And he said, "Rita . . ." It was Leon. I didn't recognize him. He had shaved his beard before he even showed me the house. It was so strange—he would have been fine with a beard in California. I thought to myself, If you were going to do that, why didn't you do it in Memphis?

I was beginning to get a sense of who Leon really was. He wasn't the guy prancing around the studio in control of the session and being adored by fellow musicians. He seemed terrified of the world. And that gave me a different perspective from the one I'd had getting to know him in Memphis. But any misgivings I was feeling were washed away by the novelty and thrill of having finally made it to Los Angeles, especially when I discovered to my shock that the song I'd recorded in Memphis—"Turn Around and Love You"—was at that moment a hit in Southern California. It was, in fact, the number 1 song in Los Angeles. I had no idea until I got to LA, and it was being played all over the radio. That certainly worked for me after having had so many of those Nashville guys say, "You just don't have what it takes to be a star."

Thanks to "Turn Around and Love You" I appeared on a lot of Southern California TV shows, so my face and name became familiar on the local music scene—which helped when I started to look for work singing in LA. In the meantime, there was seldom a dull moment living at Leon's. The Skyhill Drive house was emerging as a hot musical salon where Leon's confederates—many of them from the South and from Tulsa, like the bass player Carl Radle and drummer Jim Keltner—would converge to write, play, record, and hang out. From his work as a session musician, Leon had played with just about everyone: the Byrds, the Beach Boys, even Frank Sinatra and Bob Dylan. Just like in Memphis, where through Don and Teenie I was exposed to the scene's greatest players and characters, Leon introduced me to the cream of the LA recording scene—many of them among the most accomplished players in the world who at the moment were emerging from session work and, like Leon, beginning to carve out careers as solo artists.

Since I'd been validated by my own hit, I was confident enough to lie back and take it all in and not worry about being tagged as Leon's "old lady," the preposterous, sexist catchall that male rock-and-roll musicians, supposedly so enlightened, affixed to any attractive female in a relationship. And so as I made my first steps into getting work as a singer, I pretty much kept house for Leon and his retinue. I didn't mind if I was the housekeeper and cook, which was not unusual for a Southern girl. If I'm staying at somebody's house, I'm going to be cleaning and cooking and doing what I would do at home—it's kind of my responsibility, too. So I kept a good house and made a lot of tea, which Leon drank by the gallon, and cooked a lot of beans and collard greens and corn bread and fed a lot of musicians. It was all pretty comfortable, although I was getting more and more concerned that Leon was just a little bit strange compared to the kind of men that I'd known. God love him, he's very funny. But he was either introverted or Mr. Entertainment. There was no in-between. And when he would shut down, there was just no communicating.

Then one night, out of the blue, Leon asked me how I would feel if we had a threesome. I told him, "Well, I don't know really, I'm not sure what you mean." Then he said, "Maybe if we had Carl Radle come over, 'cause I know you like Carl." Carl and I had become good friends through Leon. And I said, "And what?" He said, "We'll all get naked." I was mortified. I said, "Wow, you're serious." I felt like Carl would be as mortified as I was. It was just so strange and I don't know where it came from except that it was apparently something that Leon fantasized about. That was the turning point in our relationship. I realized that I was probably not going to be sticking around much longer, so I got my plan together.

Leon had a white van that had the LAPD insignia painted on the side, yet another of his eccentricities, which I drove on house errands, and I borrowed it when I decided that I was moving out. I couldn't tell Leon that I was moving because I knew there would be a campaign to keep me from going, and a big scene. I'd become friends with Terri Rodgers and her twin sister, Annie, who were girlfriends of musicians living at Leon's. Terri and I are still best friends—she was a TV stylist for years.

The Rodgers twins lived with three other women in a two-bedroom apartment on Fulton in Hollywood on the second floor, no air conditioning. Terri and Annie knew I was wanting to move out of Leon's, and they had said when I was ready to leave, I could always come over there. So that's what I did—they helped me pack up Leon's van. Now there were six of us living in a two-bedroom apartment with no air conditioning.

We called ourselves the Teenage Bad Girls—we had these denim jackets with TEENAGE BAD GIRLS patches embroidered in pink on the back. I'm not sure what, exactly, we were thinking, but we hatched this group persona as superhero young women who could fight for our friends when they needed help. It was the dawn of the feminist movement, and this was our bit for the cause. Or something. One of our girlfriends, Marilyn, worked at a club in the Valley and told us she was being harassed by one of the other waitresses. We said, "You know what? We're coming out to your work tonight and we're just going to take care of this for you. Trust us, after tonight she will bother you no more." Teenage Bad Girls to the rescue!

So we went out there and we've got on our Levi's jackets with the Teenage Bad Girls patches and were looking just as mean as we possibly could. We sat down and asked Marilyn, "Which one is it?" And she pointed to this girl. And so every time this girl had to come through from the bar to the restaurant, she would have to go past us. And every time she came by, we would say something like, "Yeah, just wait till later tonight. You don't mess with us, you don't mess with our people." We kept throwing out these ridiculous remarks and the girl quite reasonably got scared and went to the manager of the club and said she was being threatened, and the manager called the cops. When we realized what was going on we said, "Well, just kidding!" and headed for the exit. But when we opened the door, we saw that not only were there cop cars but helicopters waiting for us to come out. They thought we had weapons or something. We were about to get thrown in jail and everyone was saying, "What are we going to do?" And I said, "I don't know about you guys, but I'm singin'!" There was a band playing in the bar. So I got up on the stage and I told the band who I was—I had the number 1 record in LA, after all, and everybody in the Valley, at least, knew who I was—and I said, I'd sure like to sing with you guys. I gave 'em a song and I gave 'em a key and started singing. I guess it worked because the crowd went nuts and the manager came in and said, "Well, apparently this is not what we thought it was," and sent the cops on their way. So I sang the Teenage Bad Girls out of a corner that night. That was the first and last mission. But we kept our jackets.

When I still lived with Leon he co-produced Joe Cocker's second album, *Joe Cocker!*, in 1969. He wrote two songs for Joe, and one of them, "Delta Lady," was about me: "Woman of the country, now I've found you / longing in your soft and fertile delta . . . be all mine, Delta lady." I was deeply honored, of course—no one had ever written a song about me, and then Leon wrote another, "A Song for You," which is probably one of the most beautiful songs ever written, period. But by then Leon and I were breaking up. During rehearsals at Leon's for the Cocker album—I sang background vocals with Bonnie Bramlett, which was a flat-out thrill—I met Jim Gordon. Jim was the most in-demand session drummer in the world at that moment. He was *the* guy on both coasts. He would do a session in the morning in New York and fly to LA to do a session in the afternoon. On top of that, my God, he was gorgeous. Six four, curly blond hair, blue eyes, and a smile that would light up the world. People were drawn to him—he was the golden boy. He was like Tony Curtis in *The Great Race*, a little twinkle on his tooth. He'd grown up in Burbank and was the drum major in his high school band, and he hadn't lost his wholesome, all-American-boy looks—when he played with Frank Zappa, Frank nicknamed him "Skippy." When I moved in with my girlfriends on Fulton, I started running into Jim around town or at clubs. We started talking on the phone, and pretty soon were seeing each other.

One night Jim called and said he wanted to come by the apartment. After I hung up I realized my hair was a mess, so I threw on this Afro wig—this was 1969, remember; a lot of women wore wigs then. Jim brought over a basket of food and a bottle of wine; it was really warm and beautiful outside, a romantic night, so we took everything downstairs and spread it out on the lawn in the courtyard of the building. Everything was going great. Then Jim leaned in to plant one on me and . . . the wig fell off. I was frantically trying to put it back on before he opened his eyes when I heard laughter coming from the second floor of the building. I looked up and saw my roommates in the window of our apartment, just laughing their asses off at me and my wig. I thought, My God, I'll never hear the end of it. And I haven't—they've made sure of that.

I knew Jim had been divorced and had a little girl, Amy, who was maybe three years old. Something I've always encouraged with the men in my life who have children from previous marriages, if they're not spending time with them, I'll say, "Let's go pick up your little girl and go get some pizza. I'm just a friend, not the new mom or anything." And that's what Jim and I did with Amy. I remember taking her to the Los Angeles Zoo in Griffith Park and the three of us spending the day together. He was so good with her. And at that moment I realized just how precious he was—this beautiful, darling, incredibly talented musician and man. So it was a shock when, later that year, I discovered Jim was battling demons that even he didn't fully comprehend, and that both of us would bear the consequences, Jim tragically so.

Meanwhile, I was busy exploring LA. And because the scene was still wide open, you could find yourself hanging with the most amazing people at the most unlikely venues, like the Brass Ring in the Valley. Delaney & Bonnie played there a lot. So did Edward James Olmos when he was still Eddie James and led the band the Blue Rose. And as often as not you'd find Janis Joplin there, too. Janis was a riot. She and I would just sit down and hang out. Janis would have bracelets all the way up her arm and you'd know that they had not been off of that arm since she put them on a month ago because her skin would turn all sorts of colors underneath. She drank too much than was good for her, but she never passed out; she always could communicate, she could walk without weaving, she could just hang all night long. She could drink like a man. I wasn't aware of the hard drugs until her overdose, which was barely a year away when I got to know her. She was only twenty-seven, the same as Jimi Hendrix and Jim Morrison when they passed. Janis laughed way down deep in her belly. I always love people who laugh like that. There's no tee-hee or titter; it's a real belly laugh. Dyan Cannon laughs like that. I totally trust women who laugh so deep and happily.

Los Angeles at that moment was beyond anything that I had ever imagined that it could be—and I didn't know this, but for me it was only going to get better. So many talented musicians all the same age were hitting town at once and finding one another in Hollywood and Laurel Canyon and Topanga and at the Whisky and Troubadour. Nobody was better than anybody else and nobody was trying to one-up anybody else—not on a friendship level, not on a player level, not on any level. At least not yet.

CHAPTER 3

Delaney & Bonnie and Friends

In 1969, Delaney & Bonnie and Friends were the open-ing act for the North American tour of Blind Faith, the supergroup formed around Eric Clapton after he quit Cream. Eric's friend George Harrison had turned him on to Delaney & Bonnie's music. Delaney & Bonnie had a fluid lineup, and on this tour the Friends were musicians who would in just two years change the course of rock and roll, forming the core of the band that would back Joe Cocker on his history-making Mad Dogs & English-men tour. The lineup was like a dream: The two Jims—at first Keltner, and later, Gordon, my boyfriend, on drums; Carl Radle on bass, Bobby Whitlock on organ, and Del-aney and Bonnie on vocals, with Delaney on guitar as well.

Blind Faith was a fantastic band in theory, but Eric, his former Cream bandmate Ginger Baker, bassist Ric Grech, and Traffic's Jim Capaldi and Steve Winwood weren't jelling on stage, while Delaney & Bonnie just got tighter and tighter and upstaged Blind Faith nightly. As the tour wore on, Eric became fascinated with Delaney and began sitting in with the band during the opening sets. When Eric left Blind Faith to record his first solo album in 1969, he asked Delaney & Bonnie and Friends to be his backing band. And then Delaney & Bonnie asked me to join. I was of course thrilled. We were hired to back Eric on tours of the UK and Europe in between recording sessions for the album in London and Los Angeles. Eric invited us to stay at his house, and in November we took off for England.

Since Jim and I were by then a couple, we flew over ahead of the rest of the band and went straight to Hurtwood, Eric's estate in Surrey. Eric later recalled he had an unnerving sensation that the first time he set foot in the house, it was fated to be his home. This was in the early days of post-Beatles rock stardom, when musicians like Eric could afford to live in estates outside London but still dress and behave like the counterculturists most of us still devoutly believed we were—blue jeans and limousines.

The day after Jim and I got there, somebody brought out sunshine acid—and not just any acid, but Owsley acid, some of the purist and strongest ever made. I'd tried acid at Florida State—as an art student it was practically compulsory—but just tiny little corner pieces, never a full tab. I was already pretty sure I wasn't a candidate for hallucinogenic drugs, but that's what people were doing then. I knew from my little bit of experience with acid that I couldn't be inside because I would get really claustrophobic and things would jump out at me. But outside? It was just beautiful.

So Jim and I got up in the morning, dropped our acid, and headed out through the countryside, led by Eric's Weimaraner. As the drug came on we just gave in and followed the dog wherever his nose took us. None of Eric's neighbors seemed to object to us wandering onto their property or visiting their barns. There was one with a pile of hay that we decided we needed to jump into but discovered too late was actually covering a pile of potatoes. But otherwise it was a day of adventure and positive vibes, the textbook "good trip." It was just getting dark when we got back to Eric's house—I was still quite high—and discovered that while we'd been out, Delaney and Bonnie had arrived. The house was brimming with their manic energy. They were such forceful personalities at all times, and now I was about to encounter them in the grip of the most powerful drug experience of my life in a strange house in a foreign country. I walked into the living room. Bonnie was perched on the end of a sofa, talking a mile a minute as always. Except she wasn't Bonnie—what my acid-soaked brain instructed my eyes to see was not Bonnie but this big pink chicken. And instead of talking she just *bawk*ed! and *Bawk!* I turned to Jim to say I needed to go back outside—I knew I couldn't handle being inside another second . . . and Jim turned into this giant, terrifying bird of prey peering down at me. *And his wings were flapping. . . .*

As frozen with fear as I was, I somehow recognized something significant in that moment that I should have heeded but didn't until it was too late. Because all of a sudden, for the first time, I was kind of scared of Jim. One thing about acid: it opens a lot of windows and perceptions about things and lets your intuition flow freely. It was telling that my vision of Bonnie was as a beautiful bird—okay, a chicken—but I love birds. (There are seven Cherokee clans—my mother's people were Bird Clan.) And it was equally telling that Jim transformed into a bird that I perceived as a mortal threat. It had always struck me that something behind Jim's smile was not genuine; I'm suspicious of people who when angry or frustrated will suddenly put on a pretend face. I was beginning to realize that Jim hid behind a lot of those pretend smiles, and it was starting to really bother me. No wonder that in my hallucinatory state Jim turned into a hissing bird of prey when at that moment he was probably smiling his charming smile at everyone in the room, including me. Coming down from that trip was the reason I never took acid again. No matter how great it is—and the good parts of that day at Eric's became a precious memory—the going up was not worth the coming down. Everything just felt like so much energy and so many molecules and

I could see them all and feel them in my body and Jim's body after we went to bed.

The tour and rehearsals made up for it, just to be that young and around people with so much pure, raw talent. Delaney and Bonnie—all of us in the band, really—were a revelation to Eric, who was used to sitting with a Robert Johnson and trying to sing "Good Morning Little Schoolgirl." I remember Delaney being impressed by Eric's collection of blues records, but I don't think nearly as much as Eric was impressed by Delaney, who'd grown up listening to that stuff and knew songs that Eric had never even heard. So, it was kind of a mutual admiration society. Plus, we were all from the South, where so much of the music Eric venerated was conceived: Delaney and Bonnie were Southerners, I was a Southerner, Bobby Whitlock was a Southerner, Carl Radle was from Tulsa—Jim Gordon, from Burbank, was the odd duck out in more ways than one. But mostly we were Southern people. It was the real deal. Eric wanted that on his first solo album so he could establish a musical identity distinct from his work with Cream and Blind Faith, and we brought it and had a ball doing it, too. That's as happy as I can remember being in my life: doing background vocals with Bonnie Bramlett on an Eric Clapton record? My goodness.

Eric was so impressionable. He heard Delaney's music and basically said, I want to do that. And Eric had enough clout that he could do anything he wanted.

He paid for our plane tickets and bought amps for the guys—he even bought Bonnie's dress for a gig at the Albert Hall. I think that after being a part of all these huge bands and having fans scrawling CLAPTON IS GOD all over the King's Road, he just really wanted to *be*. Delaney was shrewd enough about people, even someone as famous and powerful as Clapton, to say things to them no one else would dare. At the start of rehearsals, Delaney said to Eric, "All right, I'm the king and you're the prince." And that's where Eric wanted to be at that time. He didn't want to be the guy who was taking over the show. He didn't want to be God anymore. I think he preferred to be a prince, and Delaney knew that was what he wanted to hear. That he didn't have to drive the bus, didn't have to be the leader.

Delaney was charming right down to the dimples in his cheeks. He was like a baby boy, he was so cute, and the women went after him like crazy. He did everything with a smile on his face, but Delaney was a force. Nobody crossed Delaney. Everything went his way. He really was the king. I was a part of so many sessions at that time where people would come into the studio and instead of having a specific plan would say, "Okay, we'll just show up and figure it out." But it ended up taking months to make those records because it was so self-indulgent—everybody's record cost $300,000 to $400,000 to make, and if it was a hit, it was paid back and you were in the money really quick, but if not, it was charged against your royalties. That's not how Delaney worked. When Delaney & Bonnie and Friends went into the studio, the musicians plugged in and it was immediate, incredibly tight music with solid arrangements. Everything was done in advance. Delaney had his plan, and everybody knew it.

Delaney came from Mississippi, Bonnie from outside St. Louis. They met when Delaney was playing a gig at a bowling alley with Leon and the Shindogs. Bonnie came from some rough stuff; she is a survivor and one of our greatest talents to this day. There is no white singer like Bonnie Bramlett, never has been. Nobody can touch her. She could have been a little blond model but instead she was born with this incredible voice. She was the cutest, skinniest little thing and just sang her butt off. Delaney was the real thing, too. People were fascinated with their talent. Later, I remember being at Elektra Studios in LA recording Delaney & Bonnie's only album for the label. The Rolling Stones were dropping by the session because they were finishing "Gimme Shelter" and wanted Bonnie to record the "It's just a shot away" answering refrain to Mick Jagger's vocal. Bonnie apparently woke up that morning and didn't have her voice—some say that Delaney refused to let her record the song—so Merry Clayton, one of Ray Charles's Raelettes who I'd worked with singing background vocals on some of Ray's sessions, got the job. Merry's duet with Mick on "Gimme Shelter" is one of the greatest rock vocal performances ever, but

I can't help but wonder what Bonnie would have done with that part. She would have blown the roof clean off the studio singing that one. When we played the Albert Hall with Eric during the tour, Bonnie just tore it up. She was wearing the long, crushed red velvet dress Eric had bought her and snakeskin boots that came up over her knees. And she pulled that dress up and started dancing and flipping the mic stand back and doing every James Brown move that she knew. And people just went crazy. I think Dave Mason, George Harrison, Delaney, and Eric all were playing that night. The next morning, on the front page of the newspaper, it said MAE WEST ROCKS THE ALBERT HALL. They weren't mentioned, it was all Bonnie. And she said to me, "Ritar, you seen the pay-perr?"

She and Delaney married seven days after they met because when they came together it was so powerful. Sharing the love and the passion that they had for each other extended into their music, which is what happened with me and Kris. If you ever have that kind of love in your life, you're lucky. Even if it doesn't last but eight years—as it did for Kris and me—so what? At least you had it. Most people don't get that. At the same time, it can be as bad as it is good. I know that Bonnie was way, way sadder when that marriage ended than Delaney was. Bonnie really loved Delaney. She loved the music, but she loved the man, too. I think that Delaney probably was more in love with Bonnie's talent, which is hard to believe because Bonnie is one of the brightest, funniest women on the planet. For all his charm and talent, Delaney had a mean streak in him, especially when he drank. One day on tour with Eric we were celebrating Bonnie's birthday. David Anderle, who'd produced Delaney & Bonnie's second album and later became my producer, had sent her roses. And Delaney misinterpreted that as David coming on to Bonnie, which was ridiculous because it was her birthday. I remember that turning into a bit of a brawl between them—I was around for way too many of those.

A few months later, when we were back in LA after the tour, Bonnie and I went out for a night on the town. There were all these little clubs on Santa Monica Boulevard at the time, and most of them had a piano. So Bonnie and I just started making the run down Santa Monica. We would go in and sit down and she would play or I would play and we would sing two or three songs and have a drink and then we'd get up and go to the next one. We had so much fun that night. When we got home I walked her up to the door because we never knew what kind of shape Delaney was going to be in. He was so inconsistent, depending on the amount of cocaine and alcohol he'd had. He was such a mean drunk, and cocaine gave him the power, the lack of inhibitions. So if he was drunk and coked up, it was trouble. I saw more than one black eye on Bonnie over the years.

So when we walked into the house that night, I opened the door, and I said "Heyyy . . . Delaney." He was standing there with his fists balled up and daggers coming out of his eyes—I thought they were going to bleed, he was so mad. He looked at both of us. Then he looked at Bonnie and seethed, "You're in so much fuckin' trouble." And I said, "No, no, no, no." And he said, "You get outta here—this is your fault." I tried to get Bonnie away from him but Bonnie shoved me into the bathroom and said, "Go out the window—get in the car and leave." So I climbed out the bathroom window, got in my Volkswagen, and went back to my house in Hollywood. And by the time I got home and turned on the TV, it was on the news that Delaney's mother, Mamaw—she lived with them and took care of their children when they were on the road—had called the police to come and get him because he was beating Bonnie so badly Mamaw thought he was going to kill her. When I finally got through to her at the hospital the next day, I said, "Bonnie, Bonnie, Bonnie, I'm so sorry! How are you?" And all she could say through her swollen—God love her—battered lips, in this tiny, wounded voice that sounded so unlike her, was, *"Don't call me no more, Ritar."*

I didn't see her for a while after that. Delaney didn't want us to see each other. I was somehow a threat to him, and if Bonnie and I were to spend time together, she was afraid he was going to hurt her or maybe both of us. So she was trying to protect me from him as well as prevent a repeat performance. It was horrible. They were married and they had children, and he would do this to her again and again. And nobody stepped in, because most of it didn't happen in public. It reminded me of that night back in Memphis when Tina had taken off her wig and showed me the scar from the beating Ike had given her. Delaney, like Ike, was a charmer—if I hadn't seen that scar on Tina's head, I might have thought, Well, she's just exaggerating; he's probably not that bad. A lot of men who control women with fear make sure that nobody is around to see it. And if you do see it, then there's always the threat of *If you tell anybody, this is going to happen to you, too.*

I don't know how Bonnie so threatened Delaney that he felt the need to beat her. I do know the thing she cared most about was singing and having that band and being able to work with him. But there were nights on stage when they would sing "When this battle is over, who will wear the crown?" and it was as if they were singing that battle between them. The audience would be going crazy, and all I could think as I watched Delaney sing those words was that he really meant: You wait till we get back to the hotel, and you'll see who's gonna wear that crown. And I would think, Oh my God, I hope this isn't going to be one of those nights. Because I think he means it.

George Harrison was also a champion of Delaney & Bonnie and came to Hurtwood while we were rehearsing, bringing along Pattie Boyd, his stunning wife, a former fashion model who'd been a fixture of Swinging London in the midsixties. George and Eric were best friends and collaborators—they co-wrote Cream's "Badge," and George played rhythm guitar, uncredited. But along the way Eric had fallen deeply in love with Pattie and was pursuing her despite his misgivings about betraying his friend. The torture of his unrequited love and pressures of fame had by then led him down the path of his blues heroes to an increasingly debilitating heroin habit.

Eric was definitely on heroin at Hurtwood because it was noticeable in rehearsals. He was in a different zone—I didn't see him really connecting honestly with anybody. And on top of the smack, he was drinking heavily. When you get to a certain level of inebriation, nothing happens: put the edge on, take the edge off, put it back on. The rest of us were maybe having a beer or smoking some hash, but nothing like Eric was up to. With most bands that I've been with, including Delaney & Bonnie, when it came down to working, you worked. And when the work was done you could do whatever you wanted. But we were all staying at his house, and it was a great big deal that Eric was going to tour with us. So who was going to tell him to stop?

As far as Eric's pursuit of Pattie, it seemed to me that when George and Pattie came around to Hurtwood, she was the instigator. Bobby Keys, the saxophone player— I'd met him in LA as part of Leon's posse of players—and his wife, Judy, were friends with George and Pattie, and one night when I was visiting them, the Harrisons invited us over for dinner. That evening, Pattie pulled me and Judy aside in the kitchen and told us that she was madly in love with Eric. I told her, "Are you out of your fucking mind? My God, you're married to George Harrison." We were all so smitten with George, this Beatle with those big puppy-dog eyes. He was so, so nice. He wasn't a peacock, he was just a nice man who had nice manners. But Pattie insisted that he was a notorious womanizer. Well, he never once came on to me, not even slightly. Maybe I wasn't his type. But I never saw that with George, ever, and I was around him a lot during the tour. Of course, it could have been going on—you don't know what's happening behind closed doors. But from where I sat, it was a really big mistake to leave George, which Pattie eventually did, for Eric. Because he was a smack addict. He was pretty, but he was gone.

Despite the heroin, Eric could always play—in fact, he played like a million bucks. How the heck he did it, I'll never know. He could play his ass off and barely stand up. He could always bring it at the concerts no matter what. We toured in Germany first as a warm-up for the UK shows—the band's final lineup was Eric, Bonnie, Delaney, who played guitar in addition to singing lead vocals with Bonnie, Bobby Whitlock on keyboards, Carl Radle on bass, Tex Johnson on congas, Bobby Keys and Jim Price (soon to record and tour with the

Rolling Stones) on horns, Dave Mason on guitar, Jim Gordon, and me. More than Blind Faith, this truly was a supergroup.

Not that that mattered to the German audiences, as we soon discovered. Because of the way the tour was promoted, they thought that Eric was headlining the concerts and so were understandably disappointed when he didn't step up and sing his Cream hits. In Cologne, the whole auditorium started bellowing "Clahp-ton! Clahp-ton! Clahp-ton!" Eric tried to explain—in English, of course—"No, no, this is not my show, I'm just playing guitar." The next thing we knew the audience was booing and ripping the seats out of the floor and we were being hustled off the stage. When Delaney protested that we hadn't finished playing, they said, "No, you have to get on the bus now." We barely made it onto the bus before it was surrounded and started careening like a ship in a rough sea. We were all thinking, *We're going to die because of Clahp-ton! Clahp-ton!* Not that we'd exactly gotten a warm welcome of our own. Everywhere we went, we were seated in the back of the restaurant because Americans were not loved at that time in Germany. We'd order eggs for breakfast and they'd serve them raw. I wanted to say, "But we're with Clahp-ton! Clahp-ton!"

The tour of England—where Bonnie had her triumph at the Albert Hall—was much better received. George jumped on the tour with us for a while. It was so low-maintenance. You'd go to sound check, do the show, and then after the show, we were back on the bus or in someone's room singing again, just hanging out and having the best time. To get on the bus every morning and have George Harrison sing to me, "Lovely Rita, meter maid ..." I'd think, Oh my God, my life is so good. Before the tour I remember walking down the King's Road, which at the time had shop after shop selling the most incredible hippie attire, things that nobody in the States had seen. And everybody in the London music scene wanted to meet Delaney and Bonnie. One night we all went to Robert Stigwood's house—he was Eric's and the Bee Gees' manager and a rising rock entrepreneur. (Little did I know that a year later, "Stiggy" would become my bête noire.) Ginger Baker, Eric's former Cream bandmate, was there, and at some point in the evening started hurling his glass into the fireplace when he finished a drink. It was my first exposure to the British rock star decadence, then in its infancy—the post-Beatles stars like Ginger were far more rambunctious and entitled than, say, the courtly George Harrison. I had never seen musicians behave like this. I wanted to say, "What is wrong with you people? What did your mother teach you?"

During breaks in the tour we worked on Eric's album at Olympic Studios in London. When the tour wrapped we returned to Los Angeles to continue recording at Village Recorders. We were all exhausted but the time on the road had made a tight band even tighter. We finally came together in that magic combination around Eric's album, which has so many of what would become his signature songs. "Let It Rain" was cowritten with Bonnie, supposedly, on the bus in England (more on that later). Delaney's and Eric's "Bottle of Red Wine" was one of six of their collaborations on the album. Probably the best example of how we influenced Eric is "After Midnight," which became the album's hit single. Credit Delaney for exposing Eric to the music of JJ Cale, then an obscure but enormously talented guitarist and songwriter. Like Carl Radle and Leon, who also appeared on the album and cowrote "Blues Power," JJ was originally from Tulsa and had played with Leon as a teenager in Leon's first band, the Starlighters. "After Midnight" was the first of several Cale songs, including "Cocaine," that Eric would cover over the years; with Delaney, he rearranged "After Midnight" from whispery blues into a pile-driving up-tempo rocker. That song was one of the most perfect examples of recording in a studio while bringing all of our roots experience to bear. We knew every trick in the book. Those "gonna let it all hang out"s that answer Eric's singing on the verses? It sounds like ten or fifteen people and is as loud—even louder—than Eric's lead vocal. But in reality it was just me, Bonnie, and Bobby Whitlock. We would switch parts as we built up the track—Bonnie would take my part and I would take Bonnie's and Bobby would take hers, so that the same voice would be singing in different voicings. Delaney would overdub our parts several times, a technique called stacking the vocals, which makes for a really thick sound with lots of depth.

Putting the background vocals on "After Midnight" so far forward in the mix—that's Delaney's roots in gospel music showing. In gospel, the choir takes the lead and occasionally a soloist steps forward to sing—that's the "step out" vocal. The body of the singing is the choir, and then you'll have a step-out vocalist who will riff or sing for a little bit in front of the choir. That's why "After Midnight" has such a strong gospel feel—in most rock music there's a lead vocalist and background singers, but with that recording, Delaney turned it around and made the background vocals as prominent as Eric's singing—in effect, he became the step-out vocalist in our impromptu choir.

It was always so much fun because we recorded every-thing live. You took the best take. If you did twenty takes, you said, "Okay, now we've passed it, we've already got it. Let's do one more for safety." The only reason there would've been a take twenty-one was because we had so much fun doing it that we just wanted to do it over and over and over. This was long before you could "fly" any-thing in or nip and tuck and edit the way they could ten or fifteen years later. It had to be there. That was the magic of recording live music—everybody playing together and bouncing off of one another. I'm sorry for artists today who have never experienced it.

Six months after the sessions wrapped in LA, the

recordings from the collaboration between England's finest and most famous guitarist and the relatively unsung players from America's South hit the street. Given Eric's self-effacing sideman's role, it's fitting that a live album from the UK tour arrived first, in March 1970. Delaney & Bonnie and Friends' *On Tour with Eric Clapton*, recorded at Croydon in the thick of the tour, is still stunning fifty years later—I never get tired of listening to it, both for the amazing playing and singing and because I'm immediately taken back to one of the happiest moments in my life. That album became Delaney & Bonnie's best-selling record, going gold and spawning a hit single, a cover of Dave Mason's "Only You Know and I Know," that Bonnie and Delaney flat-out nailed.

Five months later, Eric's solo album, *Eric Clapton*, was released and "After Midnight" was blasting out of radios everywhere. It was such a thrill to hear my voice alongside musicians I loved and admired, especially when I knew how deeply we'd affected Eric's playing and musical point of view. Under Delaney's influence he had blossomed as a singer—before, he'd always let others, like Cream's Jack Bruce and Blind Faith's Steve Winwood, handle most of the lead vocals because he didn't like the sound of his voice—crazy, because it's so intimate and expressive. Critics noted—not always approvingly—that Eric had changed his style of guitar-playing: he'd replaced the Les Paul and SG guitars that he had played on Cream's big hits with a Stratocaster, Jimi Hendrix's favorite guitar, which has a brighter, crisp tone and is favored by R&B and country players. His solos, which had become legendary for their length and virtuosity, were shorter, more lyrical, and woven into the emotion of the song—Delaney's influence again. At the time, Eric, desperately in love with Pattie, was in emotional agony; it's a testament to Eric's sheer will, the depth of his talent, and his love of, if not himself, then his music, that he could make such beautiful music under such conditions.

Incredibly, in August 1970, just as *Eric Clapton* was released, he would gather the heart of Delaney & Bonnie and Friends—Carl Radle, Jim Gordon, and Bobby Whitlock—at Miami's Criteria Studios and record a suite of songs about Pattie that exposed every last fiber of his aching heart for her and all the world to hear, including the song that would become the album's—and Eric's—masterpiece.

CHAPTER 4

Mad Dogs & Englishmen

The Mad Dogs & Englishmen tour—the now-legendary rock-and-roll circus starring Joe Cocker and one of the greatest ad-hoc bands ever assembled that shambled across the country in the spring of 1970—changed my life profoundly. By the end of the tour I was signed to my first record deal. But it also scarred me as deeply as my car accident, both physically and emotionally, all the more because what happened to me in a hotel corridor late one night deep into the tour was no accident. The tour was arranged at the last minute and almost didn't take place. But against all odds a twenty-five-strong entourage of singers, players, and untold hangers-on—including a groupie known as the Butter Queen and a canine that looked just like Nipper, the RCA dog—were conjured in less than a week, herded aboard a wheezing Lockheed Constellation and into history.

By March, Joe had been touring nonstop since his

galvanizing performance at the Woodstock festival, where he transformed the Beatles' "With a Little Help from My Friends" into a devastating blues showcase for himself and his crack Grease Band, old friends from Sheffield, England. The documentary of the festival, which became a tremendous commercial and cultural hit—it would earn $50 million at the box office and change the priorities of the record business forever—was only weeks away from release. The Woodstock movie would turn Joe, already a reluctant star, into an even more reluctant superstar. All of that was just around the corner—things were moving so fast in those days—but no one had a clue how big Joe, and rock, were about to become. The circumstances surrounding the Mad Dogs & Englishmen tour actually provided a preview of how the music business was changing—and how it would destroy the creative atmosphere that we innocently assumed would last forever.

Joe had arrived in LA thinking he was going to take a desperately needed break; he and the Grease Band had mutually decided to part ways and he was looking forward to relaxing and hanging out in LA's music scene. Instead, he discovered that his manager, Dee Anthony, had booked him on a seven-week tour. The itinerary was brutal: forty-eight concerts in fifty-two cities. By the time Joe found out, the contracts had already been signed and opening night in Detroit was a week away. Joe was still so young and new to the business that he innocently told his management, "Ah, you know, I don't think I want to do this." And they told him, "No, this is not if you want to—you have to." These people were serious. He was evidently made to understand that if he backed out, he would never play the US again. So he agreed.

With only a week to assemble a band, Leon and Denny Cordell, Joe's producer and Leon's partner in Shelter Records, his new label, put the word out to the Oklahoma posse. Chris Stainton, pianist from the Grease Band, signed on, which probably helped Joe feel a little less isolated. David Anderle, Delaney & Bonnie's producer, asked me to pull together a choir. To my surprise and delight, he added, "When you do your first record, I'm going to produce it." I still didn't have a recording contract, so that was quite a leap of faith. The official background vocalists on the tour included me, the great Claudia Lennear (inspiration for the Rolling Stones' "Brown Sugar" and David Bowie's "Lady Grinning Soul"), Matthew and Daniel Moore (writer of "Shambala"), Bobby Jones, Nickey Barclay, Donna Washburn, and the songwriters Donna Weiss and Pamela Polland. But in the chaos on stage during the tour, so many people who thought they were singers got behind those microphones—groupies, roadies, and hangers-on—that when it was all over, before the live album was released, I went into the studio with Glyn Johns, brought real singers in, and fixed every single track on that record.

Before the week was out, Leon—who himself would play guitar and piano on the tour—had dragooned Bobby Keys, Jim Price, Jim Gordon, and Carl Radle, plus Jim Keltner and Chuck Blackwell on drums; and Don Preston on guitar. Something I didn't process until much later was that we were, in effect, stealing Delaney and Bonnie's band, minus Delaney and Bonnie. Bonnie never called and said, "Ritar, why are you runnin' off with them?" But we weren't working at that time and were not on retainers, and Joe was in desperate need of a band. The pressure Dee Anthony was putting on him was unambiguous: the dates had been booked, the contracts signed; you will do the tour or everybody's legs are going to get broken. In our haste it didn't occur to us: *Oh, my God, Delaney and Bonnie are going to be heartbroken.* And they were. They felt like they had been totally abandoned, which I understand now. Who knows, if Delaney & Bonnie had had a hit record and had the power to go on the road at that time and keep the band working, maybe the Mad Dogs tour would have looked elsewhere for musicians.

What became evident was that the friendship and the camaraderie and sheer tightness of Delaney & Bonnie and Friends was unique. Because the Mad Dogs tour was nothing like that. We didn't choose to be together; we were thrown together for the tour. Everything about it was kind of upside-down, with everybody competing to take over the stage. But any misgivings anybody might have had were lost in the whirlwind of organizing the tour. We rehearsed around the clock, knocked out a Stax-Volt-flavored version of "The Letter," the Box Tops hit, with Joe on lead vocal, and hit the road. Just before we left, we had a group portrait taken on the A&M lot, the last great independent label, cofounded by Herb Alpert, a musician, and his partner Jerry Moss, a businessman with the soul of artist. Jerry took one look at us—this ragtag circus of musicians, wives, children, and dogs led by Leon in his big silver top hat and Captain America shirt and striped pants and suspenders and said, "Um, you know, we really need to film this." So a crew was put together at the last second to film what would become one of the first rockumentaries.

Joe was ostensibly the star of the show—the tickets said "Joe Cocker and Friends," yet another unintentional dig at Delaney & Bonnie, who'd used "and Friends" with their group's name for years—but he wasn't really calling the shots. Leon was the band's musical director and playing the role to the hilt—he was in control of everything that happened on that stage. He and I hadn't had much contact since the breakup; our relationship on the tour was strictly professional. He was brilliant, and the show never would have come together without him, but it diminished Joe, who was used to fronting his own band. Joe wasn't included as the tour was being put together—how it was going to be played, how it was going to be orchestrated, who was going to be doing what. He was simply told, "Okay, you're going to do the tour, it's going to be done this way, you just show up and sing." Joe was very smart but he was an extremely, extremely sensitive man. He was like a lost puppy, so easily taken advantage of and vulnerable to everyone around him. I was walking to the stage with him one night and people were handing him pills and he was just popping them in his mouth and swallowing them without asking what they were. I said, "Joe, what are you doing, this could be acid." He said, "Of course it is, love. The only difference in one tab and ten tabs of acid is the pain in the back of me neck."

Once the tour was underway and he hit the stage, Joe was unquestionably the star—out of everyone in that chaotic cast-of-thousands entourage, he was the most magnetic and charismatic by a long shot. Joe didn't have to strut around wearing a Captain America top hat like Leon; Joe just had the talent. Despite this, he was miserable. I'd sit with him on the plane because he seemed so dispirited and lonely. I was, too. There were so many times on that tour that I just wanted to go home. It was so grueling with all those people: do the gig, get on the airplane that held maybe fifty people, and there were always fifty-five sleeping in the aisles. And on top of that, the film crew was shooting everything—the cameras were always on. So I would say to Joe, "I can't do this. I've got to go home." And he'd turn to me and say, "You can't leave—you're the only friend I've got." I was stunned. The man who at Woodstock had held three hundred thousand people in the palm of his twitching hand, the star of a sold-out tour, confiding to a skinny background singer that she was his only friend. I guess in a sense we both came away from that tour with some injuries and some damage. So maybe that is why I always felt so close to Joe. But that's what the Mad Dogs & Englishmen tour did to us all. Nobody got out of that tour unscathed.

I was still seeing Jim Gordon, one of the three, no less, drummers that Leon had picked for the tour. If I'm in a relationship with somebody, I don't spend all my time with him. I need to feel that who I am, and who he is, isn't defined by our being together—when we come together, that's ours, for no one else, precious and private; the rest of the time we're our own people, which makes us stronger as individuals and strengthens the bond between us. So once the tour started, I spent my days hanging out not with Jim—everyone knew we were together, anyway—but with other people like Carl Radle and Donna Weiss who were friends. Jim was not always around, either, which seemed right to me. And then of course after the tour I found that he was having a thing with Donna Washburn, one of the background singers I'd recruited, who happened to have been Leon's girlfriend before I came on the scene. So maybe she was playing payback with me. It sounds like a bunch of childhood stuff. But you know, basically, we really were kids.

There was a pretty charged sexual atmosphere on the tour, to say the least. We were all so young. I was only twenty-four. So were Leon, Jim, and Joe—there probably wasn't anybody over thirty in the entourage. Also, this was, after all, 1970, and part of the scene surrounding a traveling rock show, along with the drugs, was sex. Make that group sex. One day I walked down to the lobby and there was a line of people. And I said, "Oh, my God, have I missed a lobby call?" And they said, "No, we have VD, we're all going to get shots." It was half the band. As for the drugs, they were always there, like background music that you might or might not notice depending on your interest. I was never much of a drug person, which probably put me in the minority.

Since I'd hit LA, I did notice that the drug menu was shifting from pot and LSD, which put people in a sharing mood, to cocaine, which had the opposite effect. Once coke came into the picture the scene was never the same again. It wasn't mellow and it wasn't fun and it wasn't friendly and relaxed. It was people grinding their teeth and not being there for one another, because that's what coke does. It really does take away your humanity, those qualities that we revere and love in one another. Bobby Keys had stashed some cocaine at his apartment in the old John Garfield estate in Hollywood—I would move there after the tour—and somehow it had disappeared while he was on the road. When Bobby came home from the tour and discovered it missing, he decided that Jim Gordon had come into the house while he was gone and taken it. I don't know if that was true, but it was typical of what coke was doing to musicians who had been close friends for so long. People just lost their moral base. It made criminals and liars and thieves out of people who had previously loved and trusted one another.

Pretty soon coke was everywhere, and it was being supplied to musicians through their producers and even record labels. There was a time when you could walk onto the A&M lot and go into almost any office except Jerry's or Herb Alpert's—they didn't do it—and somebody would pull it out and offer you some. I did an album with a producer who managed to bill his cocaine charges to my album costs. It was to the tune of $30,000. And I said, "What is this?" I didn't know that you could do that, but apparently you could. Guys wore little coke spoons around their necks on gold chains. It was kind of an insidious time—the medical community was saying that cocaine was not addictive and all the things that everybody wanted to hear, because people could work around the clock when they were on it and produce more "product," as records were increasingly called. And that's something else about drugs like coke—although they make everything happen a lot faster, it doesn't mean that it's real.

After each show on the Mad Dogs tour, a lot of nights the people who were not participating in the orgies or whatever else was going on would still be so full of music that we would go to somebody's room and pull out the guitars and sing for another hour, or smoke a joint and watch Johnny Carson. We were in Carl's room one night after a show, and it was really mellow—everybody just kind of laughing and talking. Jim was there, too, and I felt really comfortable and safe with him that night. It was a respite from the stress of the tour to be among friends and close to my boyfriend, especially having been on stage with him an hour before, both of us playing and singing our hearts out. I'd never felt closer to him or more in love. And suddenly Jim said very quietly, so only I could hear, "Can I talk to you for just a minute?" He clearly meant he wanted to talk alone. And I said, just as quietly, "Yeah, sure." So we walked out of the room together—it was late at night, the hallway was deserted—and he closed the door. It was just the two of us. It wouldn't have shocked me at all if he had said, "When we get home, could we get married?" That could be the reason he wanted to be alone. To propose. He was, after all, a romantic, in his shy way. That was my state of mind as I stood there with him—a little nervous, but in an anticipatory way, the way you feel when you think someone's going to give you a really nice surprise—or maybe a first kiss. So I stood there with him, waiting.

And then he hit me so hard that I was lifted off the floor and slammed against the wall on the other side of the hallway.

He'd hit me in the eye and briefly knocked me unconscious. Jim's a big, big guy: broad shoulders, drummer arms, very strong. His upper body was very built; he could be his own umbrella with those shoulders. And I'm one hundred pounds. So when he hit me I literally went flying. When I came to and realized what had happened, besides the pain, the true shock was that he'd hit me. Nobody had ever hit me before, ever. As a child, I wasn't even spanked. The next thing I know, one of the other background singers, Nickey Barclay, was dragging me into her room. When Jim struck me, I had hit the wall of the room she was in, and she came out and found me crumpled on the floor of the hall. Jim was gone. Apparently he had walked back into the room and sat down like nothing had happened. "He just came back and you weren't with him," Carl told me later.

Somebody called Smitty, the tour manager. Sherman "Smitty" Jones was this incredibly regal black guy who could sweet-talk a Holiday Inn line cook into whipping up vegetarian meals for the entourage at one in the morning. Smitty was like my dad—he could do anything; he got things done and made everybody happy. He spontaneously recited the entirety of the epic poem "The Face Upon the Barroom Floor" for everyone's amusement during a picnic near the tour's end. Anyone who could keep the Mad Dogs tour functioning is someone you definitely want nearby in an emergency. By the time Smitty came down my eye was already swelling. It was one of those black eyes where the eyeball is all red, blood inside, with a big purple shiner surrounding it. They took me to the hospital but there wasn't anything they could really do. I didn't have a concussion. They just said to ice it.

Well, the show had to go on—there were still two weeks left of the tour. Plus I had a solo spot singing "Superstar," a song I'd written with Bonnie during Eric's tour that would later become a wedge in our friendship, and now I had to perform it with a huge purple bruise covering half my face. I didn't file battery charges against Jim, but I did sign a restraining order. And Smitty made sure I was safe for the rest of the tour. He would come to my room every night and escort me to the gig and bring me back to my room at night and make sure that I was with somebody so that Jim could not get near me; the rest of the band formed a kind of wall of protection around me. It wouldn't have benefited anybody to have a lot of people taking sides. The object was to just keep Jim away from me, and to keep me protected so that I could function for the rest of the tour.

That empty look of Jim's I'd first noticed in England was growing more and more prevalent as the tour ground on. It was chilling—there was no light, it was pure darkness. He was doing a lot of coke—if he, in fact, stole Bobby's stash from the Garfield house, he would have had an ounce or so, an immense personal supply—so when his mood would shift so suddenly and violently, I figured it was the drugs. What nobody knew at the time about

Jim, however, was that he was an undiagnosed paranoid schizophrenic, and the symptoms of his disease, probably exacerbated by the drugs he was taking, were becoming increasingly hard to conceal. He was hearing voices. And, gradually, he just went away—the golden boy with the twinkle in his eyes was gone. Five years later, those same voices that had likely told him he should hit me as hard as he could commanded him to enter his mother's house and bludgeon her with a hammer; when the hammer failed to kill her, he switched to a carving knife. He was convicted of murder and is serving a life sentence at a psychiatric prison in Vacaville, California. In 2013, his attorney's most recent request for parole was denied—in part because Jim resists taking his antipsychotic medication, according to the parole board's decision—and he won't be eligible again until 2018.

At the last concert on the tour, in Santa Monica, when I knew A&M was going to be there to see me perform in my solo spot, I still had my black eye. Everyone on the tour tried to reassure me: Oh, they don't care about that—besides, it matches your red shirt. After the concert, A&M's Chuck Kaye came backstage and said the words I'd been hoping to hear since I left Memphis with Leon: "We want to sign you." So it was a triumphant way to end the tour.

As soon as I was off the road I went to the doctor because I was so thin, from all the stress and irregular meals and lack of sleep. And of course, I still had the remnants of the black eye. The doctor said, "You need to drink a malted at least once a day—you're verging on malnutrition here." I looked like a refugee, a rock-and-roll refugee. I was so physically and emotionally beat up and plain exhausted, I needed to step away and build some strength, get some distance.

Joe ended the tour in terrible shape, too. Despite being forced to perform night after night when all he wanted to do was rest and recharge, he was virtually penniless. He called me and said that he was sleeping on the floor at Denny Cordell's. He didn't have a pot to piss in. All the money he should have made as the star of the tour had gone to the production, the airplane, and however many people it was on the road. It was scandalous that the man who had given so much of his talent and soul to that tour—which of course wouldn't have happened at all without his drawing power—should be treated so shabbily. Priscilla and Booker had moved to LA and were renting a house off Crescent Heights by Wilshire. I was staying with them for a while after the tour, so I would take Joe over to Prissy and Booker's and he would spend a couple of days and get some sleep. I wouldn't say we were romantically involved—I just wanted to take care of him. We'd lie in bed and just hold each other. I'd cook for him and help him get his head clear. Then I'd take him back to Denny's house in the Valley.

When the film of the tour was finished months later, we were all invited to a screening at the MGM lot in Culver City. I didn't want to go because I was still reeling from the experience—it was like after my car accident, when I couldn't ride sitting up in a car for fear I'd go through the windshield. But it would look disrespectful to the others if I didn't show, so I put on a crushed green velvet coat and black velvet dress and went. And while I sat in the screening that night and watched the movie, my whole body started shaking. I was reliving the whole thing. Not just Jim's attack, but the exhaustion and the feeling that I'd never recover from the tour. I just got up and walked out. Nobody was surprised—they all understood.

After the tour, Jim would leave books, cards, gifts on my doorstep or on my car. I never even opened them; I threw everything away, I was so terrified of him. It took weeks for the bruising around my eye to fade. But for me, it was a lifelong injury. Because I could have made it through my life without ever being hit and knocked out. That's not something that should happen even once.

CHAPTER 5

Love the One You're With

One of my favorite gigs as a background singer was recording vocals on Stephen Stills's "Love the One You're With." It was such a rousing song; there were at least six singers crowded around two microphones, belting out the gospel-style chorus. That session was also the beginning of a huge chapter in my life because that night in 1970, Graham Nash was at the studio. Crosby, Stills & Nash had just come off their first album, with Graham's hit "Marrakesh Express" and Stephen's masterpiece "Suite: Judy Blue Eyes," about his romance with Judy Collins. The session was at Sunset Sound, at the corner of Sunset and Cherokee in Hollywood, where I recorded most of my albums. Sunset is one of the world's great recording studios and, in the seventies, it was the source of so many of the era's signature albums and hits. It had a big recording room and an echo chamber that everyone wanted to use. Really comfortable, too—they even had pinball machines. During a break between takes, I started talking to Graham. He told me CSN were playing at the Universal Amphitheatre the next night. Then he surprised me by asking if I wanted to go to the concert. I didn't know if it was a date or if he was just getting me tickets, and I was too shy to clarify that. He said he was staying at Stephen's house in Laurel Canyon, gave me the number, and said to call him the next day.

But when I called, Stephen answered the phone and said, "Graham is not here right now, but he told me if you called to tell you that he's not going to be able to go with you—he's made other arrangements. I'm going to pick you up." I'd just met Graham the night before, and of course I knew their music and wanted to go to the concert, but it was a little strange—I still didn't know Graham's intentions. So I took Stephen at his word and he picked me up at the Garfield house, where I'd moved after the Mad Dogs tour, in his little Mercedes sports car. As we were zipping through Laurel Canyon on our way over to Universal, Stephen said, without preamble, "What sign are you?" I said, "Taurus." And he said, "What day?" I said, "May first." And he suddenly pulled the car over to the side of the road and stopped. And I'm thinking: Okay, what did I just do? He said, "I was in a relationship with Judy Collins for many years. She's the love of my life." He then added, "Her birthday is May first."

Stephen sat there in his Mercedes looking at me as if I

should have an opinion about this. I didn't really know what to say, so I finally said, "Well, I'm sure we're nothing alike. And if we are, it's in the nicest ways. And the fact that we're both singers is a good thing." That seemed to satisfy him and we went on to the concert. Graham was backstage after the show. He was very cool to me—I noticed that he didn't seem to be with anybody, but he wouldn't talk to me. And of course Stephen was over the top and playing the star that he was born to be, paying me all sorts of attention. Since Graham seemed so disinterested, I went out with Stephen a few times. He was actually more into pursuing me than I was into being pursued by him because I still had my eye on Graham. I thought Stephen was cute—he was little, with blue eyes and blond hair—but there was something about him I couldn't parse. He started writing songs about me—one of them, "Cherokee," ended up on his solo album ("Nothing 'round here get to me / Like the lady from Tennessee"). This was in the space of knowing him two weeks. I thought to myself: This would probably be really cool if I cared about him as much as he does about me.

From the moment I met him, I knew that Graham was someone I wanted to know, who I knew I could spend time with. And when that didn't happen right away, and I ended up going out with Stephen, it was extremely unsatisfying. Stephen made sure that we were never around Graham. So I finally called Graham and told him, "I want you to know what happened—I didn't stand you up that night." I also told him what Stephen had told me and was astounded when Graham said that Stephen had told him the opposite, that I had canceled. I put all this together and realized what a sneaky little bugger Stephen was, and that I really didn't want to see him anymore. Besides which, he drank too much. And he did a lot of coke.

Stephen used to go the Santa Anita racetrack in Pasadena and run the horses in the wee hours when the sun was coming up, and he would be coming down from whatever he'd gotten up to the previous night. And one of those mornings after I'd broken things off, I heard he went back to his motel room, scrawled something like I LOVE RITA on the bathroom mirror, and took a handful of pills. Apparently they found him in the hall and took him to the hospital. When I heard about it, the story didn't surprise me because Stephen was always about drama. I thought that he could have been making an attempt to get my attention and it got away from him. But I don't think Stephen ever really loved me. I think he just liked the idea of it because Stephen, honestly, was so stuck on himself. He just liked himself better than anybody.

It could get comical. When we played the Havana Jam in Cuba, a sort of cultural exchange concert in 1979 featuring American and Cuban musicians—"The Bay of Gigs," we dubbed it—Stephen was playing his guitar solo when he suddenly showboated his way into the audience and up the aisle of the Karl Marx Theater. He was trying to go around the back and come down the other aisle to the stage, but the only way he could get there was to go through the bathroom. So now Stephen's disappeared; you can still hear the guitar but he's stuck in this bathroom, trying to find his way out the other door. We were dying on stage; the audience must have been thinking: These Americans are really funny—they play their guitar solos in the bathroom. When I was recording my first album, Stephen came in to lay down a guitar solo. Booker T. Jones was playing, too. Stephen walked into the studio and actually said to Booker, "I think the significance of this record really doesn't have anything to do with Rita. The significance of this record is that the two great musical geniuses of our time, you and I, have met." I saw Booker's eyes getting big; he was waiting for me to come down like a wildcat and start ripping Stephen apart. But I was so amazed that I couldn't even speak.

Graham and I had meanwhile started quietly seeing each other. Graham was very much his own person, had a strong sense of who he was, and was comfortable in his own skin. He had come from success with the Hollies—he wrote and sang some of their biggest hits, including "Carrie Anne," about Marianne Faithfull—so he didn't have to prove anything to anybody. He knew that he was a good singer, that his talent was unique, and that he didn't sound like anybody else. He was also very easy on the eyes, tall and skinny, the perfect guy, at least to me, and as sweet as any human being I've ever met. He had recently broken up with Joni Mitchell—he wanted to marry, she didn't—after they had lived together in Joni's Laurel Canyon bungalow, the house where he had written about their life with "two cats in the yard" soon to be immortalized in Crosby, Stills, Nash & Young's "Our House."

I knew that he had had a very meaningful relationship with Joni; he made no bones about it—he never pretended to be anything ever except who he was. That's unusual in any man, but especially for a musician as famous and successful as Graham. He had such a great love and respect not only for Joni but for her music. Probably more than any other musician I knew, Graham had a lot of respect for my talent, not just as a singer but as a writer and as a player. Graham wrote a lot of the songs on *Songs for Beginners*—his first solo album—on the piano at my house, and he would always draw me in, asking, "Listen to this, what do you think?" And when he recorded the album, he asked me to play on it. I actually went in the studio and was the piano player on some of that record. And what that did for my confidence was really tremendous. Graham always made me feel like an equal, which is unbelievable given the egos of most male rock musicians.

When Graham and I started our relationship, we decided, or rather Graham decided, that we needed to go to Stephen's house and talk to him. He said, "You know, I can't be sneaking around because I don't want to deceive

Stephen. I don't want to cause trouble in the band. I want to be up front about this before we start spending time together. We have these feelings for each other. We're not going to do it in the dark, we're going to bring it out in the open." I don't think Graham ever looked at Stephen as a double-crosser. He just looked at him as somebody who was not as grounded as the rest of us. And he liked Stephen.

So we went up to Stephen's house in Laurel Canyon—he was renting it from his friend Peter Tork, who'd blown through his Monkees money. (Stephen had recommended Peter to the producers of the Monkees after auditioning himself and being rejected, supposedly because of his teeth.) We got out of the car and started walking toward Stephen. He was by the pool, dressed in his usual white T-shirt and faded Levi's. There were already tensions in the band; there had been since the very beginning when they sang together for the first time in Cass Elliot's living room in the canyon. Stephen was a compulsive taskmaster who loved David Crosby's voice—he had the perfect tenor that made CSN's harmonies unique—but hated David's tendency to pontificate when his drugs agreed with him. David was jovial, but he had a strong personality and stronger opinions, especially about politics. He was a wild and crazy little thing. (He's not so little anymore. The last time I saw David he was, as a friend of mine used to say, as round as a can of corn.) He actually thought I was the devil. One night at Stephen's I made a pot of beans and some corn bread. David rolled in—he'd been up for a few days, I think—had some beans, and immediately went into the living room and passed out. When he woke up a few hours later he said to me, in perfect seriousness, "You put quaaludes in the beans, I know you did—you're the devil woman." When I saw him in New York a few years ago I asked him if he remembered and he said, "I'm still pretty convinced you put drugs in my beans." (I seemed to have a talent for inviting accusations from indisposed rock stars—Gram Parsons had a seizure while passing me on the stairs at Leon's, and when he came out of it he looked at me and sputtered, "What did you do to me?")

Graham was the nominal father figure in CSN—his nickname within the entourage was "Daddy"—who'd attempt to mediate the skirmishes between David and Stephen and, as often as not, get drawn into them himself. Graham was the glue—because he was the peacemaker, he was able to reel in the other personalities. He recognized the talent and the magic that came from the blend of their voices. That's why they were together—it wasn't for any other reason except that the music was superb. It was like the Mamas & the Papas or the Delaney & Bonnie rhythm section—when certain people come together and there is a level of expertise and a passion for the music that they're making that transcends any personal differences they might experience. The Mamas & the Papas all had unique voices and together they knew how to blend them to make a unique sound. The way Crosby, Stills & Nash blended and resonated was just perfection, a sound that lasts. Plus they were great entertainers and had years of experience—David with the Byrds, Stephen with Buffalo Springfield, and Graham with the Hollies. They understood that when you're on the stage, that's not the place to air out difficulties or any tension in the band. I learned that singing with my sisters. We would sit down and Mother would play the piano and we would rehearse and these little arguments would start. I was not usually a part of those because I sang alto. But Priscilla and Linda were always snapping, "You're on my part, you're singing my note." And Mother would say, "Stop it. This has no place in what we're doing right now. You all can go in the other room and argue or we can stay here and sing but we're not going to do both." For Graham, Stephen, and David, performing was when they came together. I never saw them walk off stage pissed off.

That was the dynamic among the three of them when Graham and I walked up Stephen's drive to tell him about our affair. Graham said, "Stephen, Rita and I want to talk to you about something." Stephen seemed to consider it for a moment. Then he just came at Graham. It was a complete surprise to both of us; he just came out swinging. And Graham, of course, is not a fighter; somebody separated them and pulled Stephen off. I'm sure I started crying. I cry at the drop of a hat. I can usually be really strong for a little while, but in the end, my legs go out from under me.

After that, things really went south with Crosby, Stills & Nash. I don't think Stephen and Graham spoke to each other for a long time. But I never lived with Stephen—we were maybe together a couple of weeks, whereas Graham and I were together for more than a year. So the fact that Stephen continued to carry that grudge struck me as silly. Graham was someone I wanted to be with, who I wanted to build a relationship with. I wanted to get to know him. I never felt like Stephen wanted to get to know me; I think he just wanted to have me. He wasn't nice to me and he wasn't nice to Graham if I was with him. He just had that chip on his shoulder and a dent in his ego, which was humongous. David maintains to this day that I'm the reason Crosby, Stills & Nash eventually broke up. But the problems within that group existed long before I came into the scene.

Now that Graham and I could see each other openly, the relationship flourished. He had the capacity for great intimacy. He was made of the stuff that women really do fall in love with—a tall, good-looking guy who was kind and sweet and polite, and always opened the door for you. It was so clear that he enjoyed making other people happy. And that's a quality that not very many people have and share so generously. When I got to California,

I had this really ratty green Volkswagen that somebody had driven out from Tennessee for me, and it was pretty beat up. Graham and I were probably six months into our relationship when he called one day and asked, "Are you going to be there for a while? You're not working this afternoon?" I said, "Yeah, I'm going to be here." He said, "Okay, coming right over, I have a surprise for you."

Graham was great with gifts. I still wear a bracelet with a turquoise stone that he gave me—it's been my favorite piece of jewelry for forty-five years. He gave me an Escher print, the *Bond of Union*, that I've had restored. He never gave me flashy stuff, just things that really meant something to me. I was waiting in my little house when he came running up the stairs and said, "Okay, I want you to close your eyes and I'm going to guide you down the stairs," and there were like seventy stairs. We made our way down the stairs, we got to the bottom, and he said, "Open your eyes." I opened my eyes and there was a brand-spankin'-new red Volkswagen convertible. And he just handed me the keys and said, "Here's your new car, love, you don't have to drive that one anymore." It was just the sweetest, sweetest thing in the world. I said, "Graham, you can't give me a car, I have to pay you back." He said, "No, you don't, this is a gift. This is nothing. I want to make sure you've got a nice car." He gave me a newer, nicer version of what I already had— because he knew that I liked my Volkswagen and that I was comfortable in that little car and would appreciate a new one rather than a Porsche.

Everything was an adventure for Graham. If he were a woman he would probably be described as "bubbly" because everything in life excited him, especially when he made a plan and it came together. Crosby, Stills & Nash had a gig in Detroit, and Graham said to me, "I have a great idea, there's a train that goes all across the country. We can get on the train in LA and two days later we'll be in Chicago, living on a train and traveling at the same time and we'll sleep on the train." We'd meet the rest of the entourage in Chicago and go on to Detroit. So we got down to Union Station in LA and boarded Santa Fe's *Super Chief*, one of the great luxury trains, in its last year of operation before Amtrak took over America's passenger trains from the private railroads. Graham had booked adjacent compartments that opened up into a big suite with sofas and chairs and berths that dropped down at night—picture Eva Marie Saint and Cary Grant's drawing room on the *20th Century Limited* in *North by Northwest*. Graham had brought candles and these velvet shawls to hang from the lights to make the compartment our own. By the time we left the station in LA, it was like being in Haight-Ashbury on a train. He was just so thoughtful about those kinds of things. I don't think anyone knew who we were—there wasn't any kind of fanfare. We went to the dining car, which was like a five-star restaurant; we read books; we played music; we met people. It was so romantic. Graham was always full of those kinds of surprises.

A few months later, Graham was in the studio and I was at home in the Garfield house with the dogs. I woke up at about six in the morning having this horrible nightmare about an earthquake. I had never been in an earthquake so I really didn't know what it was, but I was terrified. And a few minutes later I was sitting in bed crying and Graham walked in the house from the session. "What's the matter, love, what's the matter?" I said, "I've just had this horrible dream about houses falling in. I think it was an earthquake." And he said, "We're not having an earthquake, everything's fine." Minutes later the dogs started freaking out and the whole house was shaking, and Graham said, "Okay, now it's an earthquake." It was February 9, 1971, and the 6.6. magnitude Sylmar earthquake, the strongest to hit Southern California in decades, was laying waste to buildings and freeway overpasses across LA. Graham and I went running out of the house and down the stairs and looked up at our neighbors' house—the steel poles that held the house cantilevered over a cliff were whipping back and forth like rubber legs.

I had a session scheduled that morning with Ray Charles. The first phone call I got was from Clydie King of the Blackberries, Ray's background singers. Clydie asked, "You okay? You going to make the session?" I said, "Yeah I'll be there, don't worry." So I left two hours before the session started because I knew that there was a lot of glass in the streets. I walked into the studio and I said, "Good morning, Ray." And he said, "Rita, darlin', what's the matter with you? Your voice sounds a little shaky." I said, "Well, there was an earthquake this morning. I'm sure you knew that." He said, "Ya know, you can't live in California and have a little thing like an earthquake shake you up." We did the session that day amid aftershocks that kept everybody on edge.

I couldn't sleep for weeks. Graham finally said, "We're going to England, they don't have earthquakes; we're going to see my mom and meet my family." And so we went to Manchester and stayed for a couple of weeks. His mother, Mary, had a pub, and there were all these people who Graham had known all of his life. I think he loved going home; obviously he was a big star, but when he went home, he was just Graham. We slept in a bedroom in the back of his mom's that was cold and damp, but I didn't care so long as there weren't any earthquakes. Before we left LA Joe Cocker had told us to be sure to visit his mom and dad, so one day we drove to Sheffield and had a cup of tea with them. They were lovely, and it was so interesting to see where Joe had grown up—his room was still the same, with all of his Ray Charles records. It was such a humble home, so much like Graham's.

Graham and I were comfortable with each other from the get-go, but I think the trip brought us closer because

I was able to meet his mother. The way a man is with his mother and how he feels about her, how affectionate he can be and how much affection he is willing to receive in front of other people—I think this says so much about a guy. Graham wasn't self-conscious about holding his mother and kissing her in a room full of people. He was very open and affectionate with her and with his sisters, and they adored him. We would go down to the pub at night and usually we would sing for a little while. And I felt like I was part of the family then, and still do. Graham's sister Elaine and I are still friends. I really, truly loved his family. I think that they thought we would always be together. And when I went back with Kris a few years later and saw Elaine, she said, "Aw, he's lovely . . . but he's not Graham."

I should clarify something about my relationships, because if you look back at this period of time in my life it might seem like I was sleeping with every guy in town. I wasn't. Leon and I were together for close to a year, same with Graham. These were serious relationships and I learned something in each one and with each one. But when the conversation invariably turned to "when we're married"— more of an implication or an assumption that we would—I wouldn't commit to a marriage, so that I could walk away. The handicap of coming from a family like mine, where my parents had this nearly perfect love for each other, is that as you go into the world, that's the standard you expect from your own relationships.

As it turned out, my siblings had already gone into marriages that fell apart. I saw that and decided not to marry young—I guess you could say I just wasn't the marrying kind, at least then. I knew that when I wanted to have a child was when I would marry. That would be more the deciding factor. And that's exactly how it happened with Kris.

When Graham and I parted, there wasn't a breakup—we simply drifted apart. We lived together for a year at the Garfield house. When I began touring, he started spending more time in San Francisco, where he'd bought a house in the Haight-Ashbury district. I didn't love Haight-Ashbury. I just wasn't as comfortable with San Francisco as I was with LA. Also, my friends were in LA, but his friends were up there—David lived in Mill Valley, which was becoming San Francisco's version of Laurel Canyon. Our relationship was never urgent or possessive; it was built on a deep love and friendship and respect for each other. I always respected the space he needed, and he respected the time I needed to be on the road and not have to pick up the phone and call home every five minutes. That's not who we were and it's not something I seek in relationships now, either. And at some point during that time I ran into that bad boy Kris Kristofferson. And after that I was totally blind to anyone else.

Graham was the best guy I ever knew. I look back at my life and think, If I could change one thing . . . I see

Graham now, and he is still such an elegant and beautiful man and his spirit just shines, his heart, everything about him. I loved Graham very deeply and I always will—and I'm sure Susan, his beautiful wife, knows that. Because I can't imagine anybody not loving Graham.

With my brothers and sisters at home in Nashville, Tennessee. *Left to right*: Priscilla, me, Dick, and Linda. (Note the records on my matching skirt and handbag.)

At the organ at Daddy's church, age seven. Music was part of my life from the moment I was born—Mother later told me I could sing before I could talk.

Daddy and Mother. Daddy was a Baptist minister; Mother was a school teacher who sang and taught her students music. They absolutely adored each other through seventy-five years of marriage. Daddy—like Mother, part Cherokee—taught me to renounce the racial prejudice all around us growing up in the South during the '50s and '60s.

My maternal grandmother and grandfather, Mama and Papa Stewart, outside their cabin in Kentucky, early 1900s.

...ewart family portrait, 1800s. Look closely at the woman fifth from the left—
...ter Mama Stewart's mother died and her father remarried a woman the children
...sliked, they cut off the stepmother's head and replaced it with their mother's.

Mama Stewart had full-blooded Cherokee relatives and was a direct descendent of Mary Queen of Scots. The Cherokee people are matrilineal, so our grandmothers were held with great reverence in our family. For Mama Stewart—a musician and artist—it was all about listening: to the music of birds, to words, to everything.

Some of my fellow students at Maplewood High in Nashville gossiped that I must be Cuban because of my dark Cherokee complexion, to which I said, "You know what? This little Cuban is going to be your next head cheerleader."

Promotional photo for my first single, "Turn Around and Love You," recorded in Memphis in 1968. The record label wanted to change my name to "Antoinette Lovely." I disagreed.

Leon Russell—multi-instrumentalist, producer, singer, and songwriter. We met when he came to Memphis to record Delaney & Bonnie in 1969. Leon encouraged me to leave Memphis with him for Los Angeles, where we lived together and I began building my career as a singer. *Jan Persson/Premium Archive/Getty Images*

Booker T. Jones, Malibu. Leader of the groundbreakin Memphis soul band Booker T. and the MG's, Booker had a profound influence on me personally and as an artist. He married my sister Priscill and created the musical arrangement of my biggest h "(Your Love Has Lifted Me) Higher and Higher." *Gems/Redferns/Getty Images*

...raham Nash in Mother's kitchen in Comptche, California, in 1970, during our ...ar-long relationship after he'd split with Joni Mitchell. Graham is made of the ...uff women really fall in love with—tall, good-looking, kind, sweet, and polite, ...ith a great capacity for intimacy. Graham had a lot of respect for my talent, ...hich was unusual among male musicians at the time; he always made me feel like ...a equal. He wrote *Songs for Beginners* on the piano at my house and would ask, ...isten to this, what do you think?"

...ith Stephen Stills in Laurel Canyon, 1969. We met when I sang background on ...ove the One You're With," from his first solo album. Graham Nash was at the ...ssion and invited me to a Crosby, ...lls & Nash concert the next ...ght, but Stephen told me that ...raham had to cancel. (It turned ...t he was lying.) Stephen and I ...rting seeing each other, but I ...s really interested in Graham. ...hen Graham told him about our ...air, Stephen had to be restrained ...a friend. David Crosby insisted ...t I broke up CSN, but there ...re tensions in the band long ...fore I arrived.

Jim Gordon, at the height of his career. Jim was the number-one session drummer in LA in the late '60s and early '70s. Breathtakingly handsome and charming, he had a smile that would light up a room—but he was succumbing to demons that would lead him to brutally attack me during the Mad Dogs & Englishmen tour and, later, murder his mother.

Michael Ochs Archives/Getty Images

With Jim Gordon backstage during the Mad Dogs tour. Not long after this photo was taken, Jim called me into a hotel corridor and struck me so violently that I had a black eye for the rest of the tour. *© Linda Wolf*

oe Cocker introduces me during my solo spot on the Mad Dogs & Englishmen
our, 1970. The historic tour was put together on seven days' notice and took a
oll on everyone. Joe ended the tour broke and broken—afterward I'd bake him
ornbread and beans and just hold him.   © Linda Wolf

elaney & Bonnie & Friends at Hurtwood, Eric Clapton's estate in the English
ountryside, during rehearsals for Eric's first solo album, 1969. *Left to right*: Bobby
Vhitlock, Eric, Judy Keys, Bonnie Bramlett, Delaney Bramlett, me, PP Arnold,
m Gordon, Carl Radle, Bobby Keys, and Jim Price. Within a year, Eric, Bobby,
m, and Carl would form Derek and the Dominoes and record *Layla: And Other
ssorted Love Songs*. Jim and I played Eric a song we'd written that, without
y knowledge or permission, would be recorded as the famous "piano coda" to
ayla," Eric's masterpiece. When the album was released in 1971, Eric and Jim
ere credited with writing the song—but I wasn't.

With David Anderle,
at the Whisky a
Go Go. I was still
a backup singer
when he promised,
"When you do your
first record, I'm
going to produce
it." David produced
my first six albums,
including my biggest
hit, *Anytime . . .
Anywhere*, released
in 1977.
Credit: Bob Jenkins

The legendary singer Claudia Lennear (inspiration for the Rolling
Stones' "Brown Sugar") and I, in wig, during the Mad Dogs
tour.   © *Linda Wolf*

is Kristofferson and I onstage. We'd fallen in love on a flight from Los Angeles
Nashville in 1971 and merged our lives and careers, winning three Grammys
ile performing together around the world. Our signature number was Kris's
lelp Me Make It Through the Night," which, when things were right between us,
sang as much to each other as to the audience.   *Credit: Bob Jenkins*

Bob Dylan, Kris, and I on the set of *Pat Garrett and Billy the Kid*, Durango, 1970
I can't remember what Bob was whispering to me here, but Kris said later that Bob
told him, "Hang on to her—she's a gem." *Credit: Bob Jenkins*

I had a small part in *Pat Garrett* as Kris's love interest. When the director, Sam
Peckinpah, wanted to send me home, Kris told him, "If she goes home, I go
home." *Credit: Bob Jenkins*

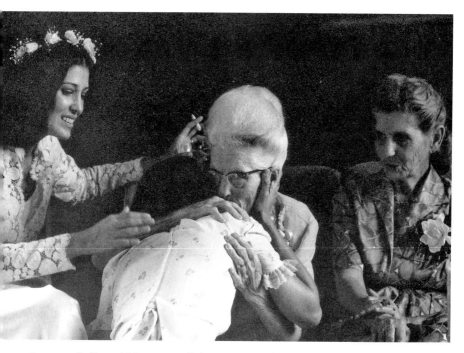

ama Stewart (*left*) and Mama Coolidge at my wedding to Kris, Malibu, 1973.

With my daughter, Casey, 1974. Kris and I had chosen her name the day we met, when we were so enthralled with each other that we knew we were destined to marry and have children.

With Priscilla, my big sister and best friend. When my face was severely scarred in a car accident at age fourteen and a schoolmate dubbed me "Rita the Teenage Frankenstein," Priscilla shrugged and said, "You're going to be the next Miss America."

With Mother and Priscilla in Malibu. Daddy and Mother lived in a house he built on Booker and Priscilla's ranch, just down the road from Kris and me.

© Jim Marshall Photography LLC

ris and I relaxing on our property in Maui, 1978, after a year headlining sold-
ut arenas promoting *Anytime . . . Anywhere*. Our hopes for a second child, and a
appier life together, were crushed when I lost the baby. Despite our smiles in this
icture, the end of our six-year marriage is months away.

home in Malibu. When things were good between Kris and me, I was over-the-
oon happy, but when it was sad, it was almost too much to bear.

im Marshall Photography LLC

Kris and I in a sweet reunion backstage at the San Diego Civic Theater, October 31, 2015, after Kris and John Prine co-headlined a concert. In the background are my dear friends Connie Nelson (with blond hair) and Ingrid Croce, wife of the late Jim Croce. *Courtesy Scott Schlumpberger*

CHAPTER 6

Layla

One afternoon in 1970 a few months before the Mad Dogs tour, Jim came over to the Garfield house in Hollywood, sat down at my piano, and played for me a chord progression he'd just composed. Most people know Jim as a drummer but he was also a capable pianist, and because he was exposed to so many styles of music as LA's top session drummer, he had a well-developed sense of melody and structure. I'd started writing songs in college—I wrote the B side to my first hit, "Turn Around and Love You"—and Priscilla and I wrote when we lived in Memphis. The chords Jim played for me were in the key of C sharp and built to an eight-note refrain before the progression repeated. There was some-thing haunting about it, especially when the bright major chords suddenly dipped to B-flat 7th for the refrain. It also seemed deeply familiar—like when you meet someone you're immediately attracted to who seems at once exotic and approachable.

I loved Jim's progression, but at the moment that's all it was—a stunning riff, not a song. As we played with it, a second progression suddenly came to me, a counter-melody in the key of G that "answered" and resolved the tension of Jim's chords and built to a dramatic crescendo that bridged the song's beginning and ending. I wrote lyrics that reflected the melody's sense of fatalism and hope ("my darling believe me, don't ever leave me, we've got a million years to show them that our love is real"). Jim and I ended up calling it "Time (Don't Let the World Get In Our Way)" and taped a demo. We played the song for Eric when we were in England with Delaney & Bonnie—I remember clearly sitting at the piano at Olympic Studios while Eric listened to me play it all the way through (so does Bobby Whitlock, Delaney's and Bonnie's ace piano player, who was on the session). Jim and I left a tape cassette of the demo with Eric, hoping of course that he might cover it. Nothing came of it, and I largely forgot about it because the Mad Dogs tour came along and then I was busy recording my own album in the summer of 1970 with David Anderle, who'd kept his promise from before the Cocker tour to produce my first record. But our song, with Jim's wistful melody and my sweet countermelody, would come to haunt me the rest of my life.

In the meantime I was thrilled to be recording my own album, though I still absolutely loved working as a background singer. In *20 Feet from Stardom* they talk about people trying to get to the front of the stage and all the hard times singers go through now, especially with everything getting looped and dubbed and the human element being lost. But there was a time—fortunately for me, right around the moment I hit LA—when being a background singer was the best job in town. And while there was certainly discrimination against women in the record business in the early seventies—it was and remains a business dominated by men, from producers to record company executives—I never saw myself as a woman in the music business. I saw—and see—myself as a human being with a God-given talent in the music business. Being a woman never got me any place I shouldn't have been, and for the most part didn't stop me from getting to where I needed to go. I don't let things force me into a place I don't want to be, and I can't be stopped if I'm going somewhere. I just persevere. It's a kind of tunnel vision I have along with—okay, busted—a lot of control issues.

I got my first big break singing background on Delaney & Bonnie's second album. That was my introduction to the studio in LA, and boy, talk about a learning curve. Because not only is Bonnie the most amazing singer, as I've mentioned, but she was just so great at voicing and at arranging parts. An important lesson I learned from Bonnie was that background singers know how to arrange background parts better than lead singers. It's not what you sing, it's what you don't sing. It's finding the right time to move behind the singer so that the background voices don't take over, but become such an important part of the song that when you're listening to a record, you're not just singing with the lead singer, you're singing with the background singers, too. Because I was both, my favorite part of making my own records later was having the singers come in, because I got to be out there with them and be a background singer on my own record, which was so much fun.

Stephen's "Love the One You're With" is one of the best examples of how to use background singers. We had such a huge choir on that: me, Priscilla, Graham, David Crosby, the Lovin' Spoonful's John Sebastian, Cass Elliot, and Claudia Lennear. Stephen was in full-on dictator mode when we cut the vocals at Sunset Sound's Studio 1 in 1970. Stephen had copped the title to the song from a saying that Billy Preston, fresh from a stint playing piano on the Beatles' *Let It Be*, was fond of dropping into conversations (he graciously gave Stephen permission to use it, after Stephen graciously asked). The lead-in to the song's chorus is Stephen-the-lyricist at his very best—his words are so good they practically demand to be shouted from rooftops, and all of us at Sunset Sound that night did our best: "Well, there's a rose in a fisted glove, and the eagle flies with the dove, and if you can't be with the one you love, honey. . . ."

The song has such a nice, loose feel partly because of the way we recorded it. When I did sessions with Herb

Alpert the background singers had their own stands and microphones and faced the recording booth. But on "Love the One You're With" we were all standing in a big circle with the microphones in the middle facing in every direction—we could see and react to one another spontaneously as we sang. Pretty soon everybody was dancing in place and wiggling and boogieing, and by the time we'd sung the song two or three times it was as easy as breathing. I didn't want that session to end, it was so much fun. To think back on it now and picture who was standing in that circle—Stephen, Graham, Cass, John, Priscilla, and me, all of us singing our hearts out for no other reason than that we loved to sing and were so thrilled to have found one another and enough success that we could make music we wanted on our terms—and you can see why I say I had the best job in town.

That Cass, who by then was a big star in the Mamas & the Papas, would make time to sing on Stephen's song says a lot. At that point we still really were all friends. It amazed me that Cass never acknowledged the fact that she was a big woman or let it affect her self-esteem—she could have been Marilyn Monroe, the confident way she carried herself. She was so full of life and always making people laugh that nobody ever thought to talk about her size, which at the time was still unusual for women and unheard of for women pop stars. It didn't matter. I saw men just fall all over her. Bobby Keys, before he and Judy got together, was just wild about Cass. He had to work really hard before she let him in and eventually they did have something going on. Cass was just Cass, and Cass was a beautiful woman.

That moment in the early seventies—when the sixties were officially over but unofficially still informing everyone's heads and hearts—was for me the golden age of rock and roll, as trite as that might sound, because it was a time when musicians still adored one another—we really loved one another. I can remember going to A&M, which along with Warner Bros., was the most artist-friendly label in town. A&M had taken over the old Charlie Chaplin studio on La Brea, which is still there. *Perry Mason* was filmed there in the sixties; it's home to the Jim Henson production company now. Chaplin had built it to look like a nineteenth-century English village, and behind the big front gate the offices and recording studios were housed inside timbered mock-Tudor cottages. It was completely whimsical, set down on the edge of Hollywood, and about as close to a perfect creative setting as you could want. I'd pull into the lot and park my car for a session, and Karen Carpenter—she and her brother, Richard, recorded for A&M—would pull in next to me. We'd have a hug, and sit in on one another's sessions. That happened all the time. We embraced one another for our talents, for our similarities, and for our differences.

The hottest background singers in LA at that time

were the Blackberries—Venetta Fields, Clydie King, and Sherlie Matthews. Venetta had sung with the Ike & Tina Turner Revue; on the Rolling Stones' *Exile on Main Street*; with Ray Charles, Aretha Franklin, even Barbra Streisand. I'd sung with them a little and was pretty much in awe of them. So I was stunned—and incredibly flattered—when they decided that if for some reason one of them couldn't make a session, I would be their substitute singer. So I became like the fourth Blackberry. My voice was not high, but they all could always move up a part; any of them could move around so that I could either be in the middle or on the bottom. Working with those girls is how I was able to get my foot in the door. I would go in to meet a producer and they would see I'd worked with Delaney & Bonnie, and then discover that I'd sung with the Blackberries, and they'd hire me on the spot.

Pretty soon the record labels and producers started turning to me not only to sing but to book the singers for sessions. Because I sang on so many sessions, I knew all the best singers and had demonstrated that I could handle vocal arrangements. So of course I'd call the Blackberries. I was glad to be able to repay them for their faith in me, plus I just loved all three of them (I'm still in touch with Venetta, who's a music teacher in Australia). But you couldn't book the Blackberries for everything— every artist demanded a tailored approach. Before we'd get to the studio I would say to the artist and producer,

"Do you have something in mind that you want to hear?" Usually they didn't, which made my job more challenging but also fun—I had to conjure from memory whose voices would blend the best with the material, the artist's lead vocals, and the other background singers, and do it fast since the calls would often come with no notice. As a cook, I knew how crucial the right ingredients were— you wouldn't want maple syrup in a gumbo or a crawfish étouffée. So I had to think on my feet: who was available, what they sounded like, could they sight-read or were they "feel" only? It got so that pretty soon, if you drew breath and sang for a living in LA, I knew you, and if you were any good, you'd get to know me. I was like the Atlanta airport: whether you were on your way up or on your way down, eventually you had to go through me.

Working with producers like Herb Alpert and David Anderle and, yes, Leon, I learned the tricks they used to fatten the sound at a time when sometimes only sixteen recording tracks were available—a third of what's used today. We'd record multiple background vocals using around five singers and then stack them so that they sounded like a big choir. I would have the guys sing the bottom part that the girls were doing and the girls sing the guys' parts an octave above.

Venetta also taught me about my voice and my craft. Take vibrato. Recording with Ray Charles and the Blackberries the morning of the Sylmar earthquake when everybody's voice was already a little bit shaky, Ray said,

"Okay, girls, when you have the *ooohs*, when you're holding the note, no vibrato." And Venetta said, "Uh, that's not possible." He said, "Just do it." (If Ray Charles is asking, you find a way.) Having to hold a straight tone for that long without any vibrato was unimaginable to Venetta. If you're holding a note, usually the vibrato's going to be in there somewhere; that's just the way you grow up singing. Vibrato's really interesting. Some people have a fast vibrato, like Dolly Parton or Barry Gibb of the Bee Gees. And then there are people like Bonnie who have slower vibratos. It can be fast or slow, it depends on how hard you're hitting a note and what you want to get out of it. Your voice is an instrument and there are so many things that you can do. I think the hardest part is making the right choices.

After I'd had my big hits—"We're All Alone" and "Higher and Higher"—one night Venetta said to me, after we'd both had plenty of tequila, "You know, the thing about you, Rita. You don't have the greatest voice. You don't have the greatest range. But what you can do with a song is why you have a hit record and not me. Because I can sing circles around you, girl. But I can't do what you can do." She said it without envy or resentment—she was just stating the facts. And I understood what she meant. It was the same with Priscilla, who'd studied voice from the time she was twelve and could sing opera. I know it was really hard for her when I started having hit records because I think Priscilla—God bless her—felt the same way as Venetta. I've no doubt that there are a lot of singers who don't like me because they think, *I sing better than her, why not me?* It's an interesting phenomenon. Priscilla could have been a huge star in the forties because music did different things then, but the way music spoke in the seventies—and still speaks today—is something that's compatible with my voice. Rosemary Butler, who sang background with James Taylor for years and is now a vocal coach, told me one night after a gig that something in my voice resonates with people's hearts, that the emotion in my voice actually travels from my heart to theirs. I understand there are people singing in Holiday Inns who have a wider range and probably sing a million more notes than me. But that's not what it takes. During those early years in LA, singing background, working with gigantic talents like Venetta and Leon and Stephen, was the best possible finishing school for my own talent. I learned that singing that is uncoupled from emotion is, as Tennessee Williams would have put it, the worst kind of mendacity. I also learned that the record business thrives on both.

One night during the tour with Eric, I looked out at this audience of young women and thought: You know, they're looking up at him and they're thinking, "He's going to pick me and he's going to take me home tonight. And then when the tour's over, he's going to come back and we're going to be together." It was the fantasy I saw on every face and it gave me the idea for a song. I called it "Superstar." Bonnie and I started writing the song in a hotel room. Delaney and Leon came in, heard what we were doing, and went into the other room and finished it. I sang it as my solo spot on the Mad Dogs tour, and Bonnie later recorded it. But when the song came out as the B side to a Delaney & Bonnie single, my name wasn't on it. And God, that really, really hurt. Because Bonnie was one of my closest friends. Bonnie doesn't have a mean bone in her body, so I have no doubt that Delaney manipulated that situation. Making matters worse, "Superstar," was later covered by Bette Midler and became a huge hit for Karen and Richard Carpenter. Bonnie and Leon eventually came clean in a 1992 *Blender* article and acknowledged that the song was my idea. And when Usher covered "Superstar," he included me in the credits (thank you, Usher). Little did I know I was about to go through the same experience with a song that would become more famous than anything Leon, Delaney, Bonnie, or I would ever record.

I was at A&M one afternoon in 1971 after I'd finished my first album, getting promotional photos taken. What a great moment that was—my album was in the can and about to be released by the best record company in the world. It was that wonderful lull before the record hits the stores and the reviews come in, when you can't do anything but wait and hope and believe. It's a moment of anticipatory tension, but also of great relief. As my good friend Aaron Neville once told me, "It's like you know what they got you for Christmas but you can't open it yet." The photographer had turned on a radio while he worked. I wasn't paying much attention but suddenly noticed that the song that was playing sounded familiar. I was thinking, Wait, I think I've heard that before. The photographer was telling me to pose this way and that, but all I could hear was that song. Suddenly, it dawned on me: the song on the radio was my song—except that I'd never recorded it. The veins must have been popping out on my neck. I cried, "That's my music! That's my music!" It was "Time," the song Jim and I had written at the Garfield house and played for Eric at Olympic Studios. Except that now it was an instrumental as played by Bobby Whitlock, Carl Radle, Eric Clapton, Duane Allman and . . . Jim Gordon—collectively known as Derek and the Dominoes. The song was "Layla." And "Time" had been appropriated as the soon-to-be-famous "piano coda" that gives Eric's greatest song its bittersweet denouement.

When I got my hands on the album, *Layla and Other Assorted Love Songs*, I looked at the label. "Layla" was credited to "E. Clapton and J. Gordon." No mention of "R. Coolidge." I was infuriated. What they'd clearly done was take the song Jim and I had written, jettisoned the lyrics, and tacked it on to the end of Eric's song. It was almost the same arrangement. I have to admit it sounded stunning. Juxtaposing Eric's desperate verses about his unrequited love for Pattie and the coda's—make that *my* coda's—wistful, winding melody with Bobby's piano and Eric and Duane's guitars intertwined with Jim's dramatic cymbal fills was a masterstroke. Following Eric's impassioned singing and guitar playing inspired by the torture of falling into a forbidden love, the coda was "nothing less than bliss, the sound of love fulfilled," a critic noted forty years after the song was recorded. Even without my words, Jim's and my original intent shines through. That didn't make being left out of the songwriting credits any easier.

I told David Anderle and A&M's Jerry Moss about not getting credit on "Layla"—in fact, I told everyone I knew. I finally called Robert Stigwood, Eric's manager. All he said was, "You're going to go up against Stiggy? *The Robert Stigwood Organization?* Who do you think you are? You're a girl singer—what are you going to do?" I talked to David and he was sympathetic but said, "You know, you don't have the money to fight this." And it was true. Also, the *Layla* album was not an especially big hit when it was released in 1970, and certainly nobody knew that "Layla" was going to become Eric's anthem. But that was beside the point—I deserved credit for my work. I never wanted the money. I just wanted my name on it. (When I later learned that Stiggy had been hung out of his office window by a fellow manager's goons to dissuade him from poaching an act, I wanted to applaud.)

There was no way Jim could have forgotten we'd written the song together. And, frankly, I don't think Eric could have, either. Despite the heroin and his general dissipation at the time, I don't think he was in such a musical vacuum that he wouldn't be able to remember me playing the song for him at Olympic. I later found out that when we were touring with Eric in England, Bonnie happened to be sitting next to him on the bus the day he started writing "Let It Rain," which ended up on his first solo album. He played her parts of it and watched for her reactions—she told me she'd maybe say, "Hmmmm." That was the sum of her contribution. But when the album came out, she was listed as cowriter. She had not cowritten the song, but Eric had been generous enough to give her credit. I wish he'd been as generous with me.

There was always something about Eric that wasn't friendly, just something about him that's kind of elitist— that entitlement thing that you see with some English people. George Harrison certainly never had it. He was the sweetest guy in the world. But Eric always has, as long as I've known him, which has been a long time. Somewhere in there, though, I think he does remember that I cowrote the second half of his greatest song. That he hasn't acknowledged it is the last little part of that experience that I can't let go. And I try not to hold on to it, because it's not going to hurt anybody but me, right?

If I sound bitter, I'm not. "Layla" has generated hundreds of thousands of dollars in songwriting royalties— maybe millions—over the years for Eric. But I know that part of Jim's share actually went to his daughter, Amy. And that, finally, was how I was able to deal with it, just knowing that she had something from her dad.

Every night on stage, before I sing "Superstar," I tell the story of how the song was written. Until now I've never told of how I helped write one of the greatest rock songs ever recorded. "Layla" has a lot of fathers—in addition to Eric's and Jim's contributions, Duane Allman may have adapted part of the song's guitar riff from Albert King's vocal on "As the Years Go Passing By." But I think it's time everyone knew that it also has a mother.

CHAPTER 7

Kris

My first album, *Rita Coolidge*, was released in 1971 to good reviews. I was twenty-five, and *Time* magazine featured me in a story about up-and-coming women in music along with Linda Ronstadt, Bonnie Raitt, and Kate Taylor, James Taylor's little sister. I was flying from LA to Memphis in November to rehearse with the Dixie Flyers—the former house band at Criteria Studios in Miami—whom I'd hired as my backing band for my first tour. At the ticket counter, my manager, John Frankenheimer—he's a big Hollywood entertainment lawyer now—pointed out a tall bearded guy who looked vaguely familiar, who glanced over his shoulder and registered that someone had recognized him and immediately tried to disappear. Too late. John propelled me forward and made introductions. It was Kris Kristofferson, who was at the time on the cusp of becoming a star after writing a string of hits for others—Janis Joplin's cover of

"Me and Bobby McGee," released after her death from a heroin overdose, had just hit number 1. That alone should have made me intimidated to meet him. Plus I could see he really didn't want to talk to anyone. He later told me that he'd broken up with Samantha Eggar the night before, and, as I soon would learn firsthand, even Kris needed a day or two between romances. He didn't have any problem with one-night flings, but when he saw something coming that might be meaningful he did need a minute.

When the plane boarded I started for my seat but saw Kris sitting in the back. "I've got a seat for you," he said. So I sat down next to him and we immediately started talking. (Kris always insists that I got on the plane first and saved him a seat. Well, I know what happened—and besides, it's my book.) It was November 9, 1971. Later I called it love at first flight, because we just talked, literally, all the way to Memphis. It turned out Kris actually knew who I was—he'd seen my picture in *Time*. That impressed me, of course, not only because he'd seen the article and remembered me, but because given our relative positions in the business, he could have just as easily played the star. That was and remains one of Kris's considerable charms—he has a mighty ego but his self-effacement and interest in others, no matter who they are or what they do, is genuine. And that, in such a good-looking man, is of course devastating. On top of which, he absolutely radiated outlaw. Everything about Kris was

Bad Boy, and that's the most attractive guy in the world to a young woman.

I felt a connection with Kris the first time I looked into those blue eyes, and it wasn't just because he was one of the most beautiful men on the planet. It was a connection that went so much deeper. As we talked we both felt an immediate kinship, that sense of being reunited with someone you'd known forever but had never met. What happens to the twin taken from us at birth? the novelist Jim Harrison once asked. The answer was you could find him—and he could find you—at the United Airlines ticket counter at the Los Angeles International Airport on a Tuesday afternoon. We both later admitted to each other that it was eerie, like we'd been waiting for the other to arrive, the way dear Priscilla told me she had been waiting for me to be born. He was familiar. You dream and you wait and you have faith and fantasies that someone is going to come along and really rock your foundation. And when he came, I knew it was him. I knew that Kris was the one. I knew it immediately. It was like a tide and it was irresistible. It was undeniably where my life was going. It was exhilarating but also calming, and, I realized, a relief: I'd finally found him, and he'd found me.

Once we commenced to talking, it was as if we were picking up the thread of a conversation we'd started years ago. We were not trying to be entertaining or cute—we really were getting to know each other. It was compulsory. We knew we were going to be together, so we figured, let's go back and get our history. We talked about our families, about where we were from; I told him about my relationship with my parents and my siblings. Kris was really forthcoming, but while I could see that this was a person who had great depth, I could also tell that he was actually very guarded. By this time, I had met a lot of cute guys who were musicians and some of them, like Graham, had a great spirit of life and openness. Graham was an open book. Kris, I could already tell, was not, and I would therefore have to tread carefully until I found out why.

From the beginning, though, Kris opened up to me completely about his family. He told me he had lost his father—Henry, an Air Force major general—a few months before, and that had been really hard for him. He was still grieving, all the more so because he was largely estranged from his family. After the usual nomadic military upbringing, the Kristoffersons settled in San Mateo, California, an upper-crust suburb in the San Francisco Bay area. Kris was a Golden Gloves boxer and football player, but he told me that he'd always wanted to be a writer—his hero was William Blake—and he'd gone to Oxford as a Rhodes scholar. After he graduated, his parents pressured him to join the military, so he became an army captain and helicopter pilot, despite the fact that his real interest was now songwriting. They disowned him when he turned down an assignment to teach at

West Point and instead moved to Nashville to pitch his songs. He took a job as a janitor at Columbia Records studios, where he met Johnny Cash, who eventually covered Kris's "Sunday Morning Coming Down." He told me his last straight job was flying oilmen to the offshore rigs in Louisiana—he wrote "Help Me Make It Through the Night" and "Me and Bobby McGee" on oil rigs in the Gulf of Mexico. (Johnny Cash swore that one afternoon Kris landed his helicopter on his front lawn and emerged with a taped demo of a song in one hand and a can of beer in the other. Kris never contradicted Johnny's version of events except for the beer—as he pointed out, even he needed both hands to fly the helicopter.) Oh, and by the way, he'd married his high school sweetheart, Fran Beer, and had two children, but he quickly added that he and his wife had split years earlier.

Kris told me all of this flying over Arizona, New Mexico, and part of Texas. That's some pretty deep sharing in a short amount of time, and the fact that he was comfortable enough with me to open up about some of his deepest, precious secrets said a lot. So we talked and talked. He was on his way to Nashville to do his first cover story for *Look* magazine. He was supposed to do the interview the next day. But we were so enthralled with each other that when the flight stopped in Memphis, he got off with me. He just said, "No, I'm coming with you." So he came with me to the house the record company had rented for rehearsals. (The band, which was already there, was pretty impressed: "Wow, look who Rita brought home.") Kris went on to Nashville the next day but stayed that night. And before we fell asleep we had named our child. We knew that we would marry. We knew that we were destined to be together. It was so powerful. I don't know how I knew but I just did. We both did.

As it turned out, I was booked to do a tour across Canada and Kris was booked at almost the same theaters, the same cities, one night ahead of me. But I wasn't selling tickets the way he was and some of my shows got canceled or postponed, so I would jump ahead and go to his shows. I had never seen him perform. I was coming from rock and roll and Delaney & Bonnie and the Cocker and Clapton tours, where the whole purpose of the concert was to get the audience dancing. Kris's concerts were the opposite. Kris would go out and sing these songs that moved people's hearts and pulled them closer together. And the audience seemed to melt into one. You could feel the sweet energy in the room. I felt it and it was overwhelming.

That was my first realization that this was what I wanted to do with my career. I didn't want to be where rock and roll was going. I didn't want to be a screamer. I wanted to move people's hearts. I had experienced that with music and church, but I think it took watching Kris perform to make me recognize it again. And that helped me remember where I came from musically. Music really is the voice of the soul and the heart. And if you let it speak to that part of you and not just the rhythms and the frenzy that it can create, that's incredibly powerful.

The tone of Kris's show was just so heartwarming. I could see why everybody fell in love with him. He was so charismatic yet at the same time like a big kid and kind of clumsy; his feet were always turned sideways, one of those "Aw, heck" kind of guys. But when he spoke to the audience he never said the same thing twice. Kris didn't have the patter; he spoke from his heart. To this day, there is not one thing polished about Kris Kristofferson. You would never call him a polished man—you had to bribe him to get him to put on a suit or a tux. His wardrobe consisted of clothes that he got from doing movies. When I met him, he had just done his first major movie, *Cisco Pike*, and I thought, Wow, he is that guy. He used to say, "With my thirsty boots and rangy hips, I'll gypsy back to you." I think that was appealing to men and women, because guys wanted to be just like him and women wanted to have him. And that's a quality that not a lot of people have.

Later, when we started recording and performing together, this powerful, powerful love that we had for each other just went right up through the microphone and onto the records and into the hearts of the audience. It didn't matter that Kris didn't sing like, say, Michael McDonald—who of course has such a smooth, polished voice. But Kris had exactly what was perfect for us. When we wrote music, when we sang together, when we performed together, it was our love for each other as much as the music that captured people's emotions. There are people today who would like nothing more than to see us together one more time. If we were in wheelchairs it wouldn't matter. They just want to see Kris and Rita together singing.

So Kris and I became a couple pretty quickly and were inseparable. When we got back to LA we moved in together. Despite our happiness, Kris wasn't demonstrative with his love the way that I expected. When we first got together, I remember being in Mexico for the filming of *Pat Garrett and Billy the Kid*, and how he fought so hard to have me there when Sam Peckinpah, the director, wanted to send me home. He said, "If she goes home, I go home." And I thought, Oh my God, that's so amazing, he really does love me. But the rest of the time I was invisible. I can remember being with him in the house they'd rented for us in Durango and just wishing he would talk to me or reach out to me—which was so strange because I knew he loved me as deeply as I loved him.

Bob Dylan was also cast in *Pat Garrett*. Kris was Billy the Kid, and Bob played Alias, a drifter-assassin. (I had a small part as Kris's love interest.) I got to be good friends with Bob's wife, Sara, who'd brought their children down to Durango during the shoot. Bob wrote and sang several songs for the movie's soundtrack, and in the middle of shooting we went to Mexico City to record "Knockin' on Heaven's Door"—Kris and I sang background on the song—which later became a top 20 hit. (Sara told me that when Bob was recovering in Woodstock, New York, from the famous motorcycle accident that almost killed him, some stoner fan managed to get into the house one night. When Sara confronted him, he mumbled, "Oh, man, are you like the 'Sad Eyed Lady [of the Lowlands]'?" from the *Blonde on Blonde* album. Sara told him, "No, I'm the woman who just called the cops. Get the fuck out.") Bob was really great around his children—the way he related to them was more natural than the way he related to adults. And despite his reputation, he could be really sweet. I remember Bob saying to Kris: "You'd better hang on to her, she's a gem."

I don't think Kris had any role models for showing affection. I remember him saying on the plane to Memphis, "If my mother could have been a general, she would have been the first female five-star general, if that tells you anything about my mother." And when I met her several months later, I totally understood. Mary Kristofferson was a hard woman with her kids. When Kris didn't accept his invitation to West Point and chose to go to Nashville instead, that was the last straw with her. If you were fortunate enough to have these grades and excel in football and boxing and to have gone to Oxford as a Rhodes scholar, and then you had an opportunity to go to West Point and serve your country and become an officer and possibly a general, then why wouldn't you do that? Why turn down West Point and say, "I'm going to follow my heart and follow this love that I have and go to Nashville"—and instead of studying to be an officer in the military, choose to be a janitor? That didn't sit well with Mary. By the time he and I met, Kris had started to visit Mary at her home in Fallbrook, California— ironically, or poetically, the town where I live today— partly to establish once and for all that the life she so disapproved of was his life now. And he wanted me to meet her as part of his declaration that he was living life on his terms, and that she should learn to accept that.

From the first time I met Mary she didn't strike me as maternal. There was no sense of warmth or physical affection. Kris had told me that the first woman he remembered telling him that she loved him was not his mother, but the housekeeper who raised him when they lived in Brownsville, Texas—she was very warm and loving with Kris. It was from her that Kris learned to at least partly trust his emotions. For all his Bad Boy posturing, he was in fact extremely sensitive when he allowed himself to be, even sentimental. He'd cry at movies, he even cried at Disneyland. And of course the tremendous empathy of his lyrics was a testament to the depth of his feelings. I knew he loved Mary and had missed her. He told me his greatest fear, after he had become famous, was that she would write a book about his life and publish the letters he'd written to her when he was at Oxford.

Now, Mary Kristofferson, like my parents, wouldn't tolerate prejudice. Kris and his family were the only

Anglos in Brownsville who attended a parade honoring a returning Latino World War II hero, something that Kris never forgot. And Mary was forever performing selfless acts of charity for others outside her family—she sent all of their housekeeper's children to college—and had a way of reaching out to complete strangers, people on the street, and showing them more compassion and kindness than she could her own children. Years later, Kris and I were visiting Stuart, my old friend from Florida State. She and her husband had an adorable baby girl who'd been born with a strawberry birthmark on one side of her face. The first time Kris saw their daughter, he took Stuart and her husband aside and told them, "Okay, this is the deal. Whatever you need for this baby's surgeries, it's not ever about money. You call me, let me know what you need. We're going to get this taken care of." He added, "I mean it," and gave them the number of his accountant. That so reminded me of something his mother would have done.

I don't know where Mary's dynamic—or dysfunction—of showing unconditional love to acquaintances but not to her own son originated. I do remember meeting her own mother when Kris and I first went to Mary's house. She was an artist and a lovely and incredibly dignified woman, and her art was amazing—there was a headboard that she had hand-carved that was so intricate, like something you would find in Bali or India. But Kris told me obliquely that she had come to this sweeter temperament later in her life. Mary was not one to talk about feelings and certainly not family affairs, but I believe that Mary's mother was probably not very nurturing to her, and that's why Mary was not ever able to show her children that she loved them. And I think that left a deficit in Kris.

Kris and I were these two really big personalities in a relationship that was always pretty volatile. From the beginning, we argued a lot. He was somewhat controlling with me, and I didn't accept that very well. He questioned me about everything. If I went to the market and was gone forty minutes when he thought it should have taken thirty, he wanted to know what I was doing, who I was with; he was suspicious of me all the time. I remember one day telling him I had run into my girlfriend, Noni, at the market—we were just hanging out, talking—and Kris accused me of hooking up with her. "My God, what, are you hot for her now?" I also pretty quickly realized that while Kris was capable of transcendence as an artist, he was equally capable of behaving like a complete shit. He was a heavy drinker and loved to smoke pot, but given the times and the standards of the music business he was hardly an overachiever. Plus he had his outlaw image to protect. And as I eventually discovered to my deepest dismay, he could not be counted upon to be faithful—which only escalated along with his fame, especially after his acting career really took off and he became a household name. Given his inclinations, and the hundreds of women coming on to him at every turn, he had, to put it mildly, a hard time controlling his appetites, especially when in the company of fellow poet-songwriters like Bobby Neuwirth, Kris's best friend. Bobby co-wrote "Mercedes Benz" with Janis Joplin. He introduced Kris to Janis and they had been an item for a while before he met me. I loved Bobby, but Kris and Neuwirth were trouble with a capital T.

One afternoon Kris left for an interview with a woman from a magazine and promised he'd be home by dinner. I didn't hear from him at all that night. The next morning he came stumbling in, obviously hung over. And I said, "All right, let me hear the story." He said, "I swear, I was at Neuwirth's house, I spent the night." For good measure he added, "You know that German shepherd that lives at Neuwirth's? I fell asleep on the floor with that dog. I've got a picture." He actually showed me a Polaroid of him and the shepherd lying on the floor together. I gave him back the picture and said, "Okay, how stupid do you think I am? You took that picture this morning to cover your ass." Those were the kinds of things that Kris and Bobby could pull out of their hats. You would think that between the two of them one of them would have given women a little more credit for some intelligence.

It was painful for me. I remember that woman specifically. I don't remember her name. I don't remember the magazine. I just remember running into her at some point later. Because after Kris and I were divorced and I would be on the road—this happened for years after—I would be doing a gig and frequently women would come backstage and find me and say, "Well, now that you and Kris are divorced you probably don't care. But he and I were together—could you tell him I said hi?" You have no idea how many women are so insensitive to their participation in the demise of a couple. Of course if they know that a man is blatantly unfaithful, then probably they're not the only ones, a fact that some of them prefer to ignore to flatter themselves. Also, sharing that information with me, they think, somehow inserts them into Kris's and my life together—they're quite greedy in that regard. And quite mistaken. It's incredibly presumptuous. And infuriating. I don't give them the satisfaction of responding.

Kris was a hard act to follow—and some of that act was not one that I cared to follow. I lost a lot of trust in relationships and began to wonder if I was better off on my own. There were times when Kris and I were married that I felt so much lonelier than I ever did living alone. I didn't marry again until I was fifty-eight.

There is a part of me that will always love Kris. We were, after all, the loves of each other's lives. As I discovered, even that wasn't enough for us to stay together. But I've never, ever stopped dreaming about Kris—nothing dramatic, just dreams of us being together. Maybe in a parallel universe, we are.

CHAPTER 8

Malibu

When I look at things that Kris and I did together and relive that magic when it was there, I'm in awe of how utterly we bonded. We merged our touring bands, recorded duet albums, and won Grammys for our performances of Kris's "From the Bottle to the Bottom" in 1974 and "Lover Please" in 1976. "Help Me Make It Through the Night," from Kris's first album, became our signature number. It was a song of such naked longing— "come and lay down by my side, till the early morning light"—that audiences would watch us, spellbound, as we sang the verses to each other as much as to them.

When Kris and I started making records together, he never, ever thought for a second that he had a great voice. He knew that he could express himself in his songs, but he used to say, "Well, when Rita sings with me, I feel like I'm singing with Aretha Franklin—I don't have to do very well because nobody's gonna be listening to me anyway." I think he was surprised that he paved the way for people who didn't have great voices, like John Prine, to say, Well, I can make a record, too. John is amazing but no one would single him out for his voice. He sure can sing his songs, though. Kris was the same way. He had a unique voice. And his voice and my voice together reflected two people and a lot of emotion and that's why it worked. That's why it always worked.

But when we were working on our own projects, we established some ground rules. If Kris was on a film, I didn't go to the set. And when I was recording, I requested that he not come to the studio. I knew that if I went on the set, he'd likely be on his best behavior, which he wasn't a whole lot of the time. I just didn't want to see that or be a party to the hypocrisy. When I was recording and Kris walked into the studio, I could feel the vibe shift and I would know that he was there. I didn't even have to see him. It's the energy that he carries with him—he's just a powerful, powerful man. Somebody in the band would see him, and that one shift in focus would affect everybody else. I would say, "Okay, stop, stop, stop, is my husband here? You here, hon?" "I just stopped by." So then we'd all have to break and spend time with Kris. It was usually a studio full of guys but they all wanted to hang out with him. Just by his being there I would lose control of what was going on in the session, and I think Kris understood that after a while. Still, it was a lot of fun when we were doing duet albums because that was just the two of us. And we had such a great time, whether we were recording in California or whether we were in Nashville—making music and being able to record where we wanted with the musicians we chose. Kris and I had a lot of freedom to do whatever we wanted, which worked just great as long as it was the two of us.

The frenzy of Kris's movie career was beginning to encroach on our personal lives—there never seemed to be a moment when he wasn't working (not that I was much less busy). But there was still a sense we were controlling our destinies—instead of the other way around—and that we could seize moments of serendipity, which were becoming increasingly precious. One day Willie Nelson and his wife Connie, who'd become dear friends to us, called out of the blue and said, "Let's get a limo and go to Disneyland." It was such an off-the-wall idea—this was around two in the afternoon on a weekday in, I think, January—that Kris and I couldn't figure out a compelling reason not to go, so we agreed. We called a limo driver who drove a lot of rock stars and announced, "We're going to Disneyland!" As it happened, I had just baked a really nice batch of marijuana brownies. So I packed those in a bag, we picked up Willie and Connie, and we headed for Anaheim, a two-hour drive from Malibu. Of course we dug into the brownies and pretty soon it was evident that they were a lot stronger than the ones I usually made, and we were, all four of us, seriously toasted when we finally got to Disneyland. It was four in the afternoon, the sun was setting, and there was almost nobody there. I can only imagine what the ticket-takers made of our little entourage arriving by limo: Willie of course was wearing his pigtails and yellow bandana, Kris was radiating stoned stardom, and all of us just red-eyed and stifling giggles. We got our tickets and headed for Space Mountain. When we stepped on the moving walkway that leads to the ride, Kris gripped the banister like it was a lifeline and bleated, "Whoa! Whoa! This is crazy!" He was so stoned, he thought that was the ride. I told him, "Kris, this is not the ride. This is the moving sidewalk." He looked at me with these huge stoned eyes, his face stricken, and gasped. "You mean it gets worse . . . than this?" Somehow we managed to get on the roller coaster and were zipping around. Willie was in the back car yelling, *"Ah-ha! Ah-ha-ha!"* every time we took a turn. When we pulled in at the end of the ride I turned around and looked at Willie—his bandana was wrapped around his neck. We were all laughing so hard that we could not breathe. Then we got back in the limo and left. One ride and we went straight back to Malibu. On days like that, with Kris and friends like Willie and Connie by my side, I could swear that we'd stopped time with our love of life and each other.

That was the dynamic between Kris and me, professionally and personally, when we decided to get married in 1973 and make a real home for ourselves after three years of living like gypsies. We were actually waiting for his divorce to come through because he had never filed for divorce from his first wife; he just hadn't seen any need to. We'd already decided we wanted to have a child and were actively working on that before we decided to marry, so we were both tickled to death when I did get pregnant. We were married in August and Casey was born in March, so I was pregnant on our wedding day, but that's not why we got married. Neither of us felt like we had to marry, although we knew we would after our first night together, in Memphis, after meeting on the plane. When I got pregnant that was the perfect time. It felt natural for us to get married and to have Daddy perform the ceremony.

Once we'd decided to marry, Kris was away almost constantly on location, so it was left up to me to find our home. We both liked Malibu. Priscilla and Booker were already there—they'd bought Lana Turner's old ranch on Winding Way (Bob Dylan's ranch was next door). Daddy built a house on a ridge on their property; he, Mother, and Mama Stewart had moved from Tennessee the year before. So I started looking and pretty soon found this house tucked away in the hills above the Pacific Coast Highway. When I first saw it I just knew—it was like when Kris and I met. I said to myself: Man, this is it. It was a ranch-style house, not at all fancy but with a panoramic view looking out over the Pacific. There was a little side yard that was perfect for a swing for the baby and lots of flowers. When Kris finally saw it he had the same reaction as me. In the early 1970s, Malibu was still underpopulated and the prices were ridiculously cheap. I think we got the house and five acres for $150,000. The sellers had built it in the forties—they were an older couple, and it was just too much house for them—and were thrilled when Kris and I bought it. We inherited their gardener and he always had vegetables growing. Friends like Gary Busey and Jeff Bridges already lived in Malibu, plus Willie and Connie had a condo by the ocean. And of course Priscilla and Booker and Mother and Daddy and my sister Linda and her husband and children were nearby and over a lot. I would go the Trancas market and Cary Grant would be there buying groceries. I mean, how good could life be?

When I went shopping for my wedding dress I was not showing at all. I would go into the bridal stores to look at dresses and of course they were all white. I'd tell the saleswomen, I don't want a white dress, I want something that's ecru or eggshell, an off-white color. And they'd say, "Why would you want that?'" I said, "Because I'm pregnant!" And then they would say, "Oh, my!" But I finally did find the dress and still have it: an ecru satin dress with a beautiful long-sleeve French lace coat that went over it. Kris wore a black suit. Cowboy boots, of course. It was hard to get Kris into anything but black jeans and a tight black T-shirt. God love him he's been consistent—it's what he still wears today.

We decided to have the wedding at Mother and Daddy's house on Priscilla and Booker's ranch. Priscilla was my maid of honor and my girlfriend Terri's little niece, Jennifer, was the flower girl. We invited all of our friends and they all came—even Sam Peckinpah. I don't think I had any illusions about my wedding night, so I didn't think Kris was going to sweep me off my feet and carry me over the threshold. That was never going to happen because we had been together for a while.

Hewing to romantic tradition, even though we'd been living together for years, Kris did spend the night before the wedding away from his bride-to-be at Roger McGuinn's house while I stayed with Mother and Daddy. We were both nervous wrecks. I was afraid that Kris would miss the ceremony, given that he was spending the night at Roger's and they definitely would not be sitting up all night drinking tea. Kris was nervous any time he had to deal with large groups of people—ironic, given how much his audiences loved him. He had to drink a bottle of tequila just to be able to deal with crowds, and in his mind my family was a crowd—all those Coolidge women. On top of which, Roger and I had some history. My first tour of England after I was signed by A&M, I opened for the Byrds, Roger's band. And the *Melody Maker*—on the front page, mind you, and on my birthday, no less—ran a story with the headline BYRDS TOUR WITH RITA. And from that moment forward, Roger McGuinn didn't have the time of day for me. When we got to Sheffield on that same tour, I invited Joe Cocker to join me on stage during my set—I'd hardly seen him since the madness of the Mad Dogs tour. As Joe and my band started jamming, Roger was pacing on the side of the stage, looking at his watch and frantically giving me the hook sign. Roger was irate that Joe was stealing his thunder, or so he thought. I was more of the mind that of course you don't want to follow him, but this is Joe's hometown and he's singing for the first time since the Mad Dogs tour, so for him to even come on stage was huge. And frankly, everybody wanted to see Joe way more than they wanted to see me or the Byrds.

So now jump to our wedding day. The ceremony was set to start at one in the afternoon. It was a beautiful August afternoon; the sun was shining, the waves crashing down on the beach in Malibu. The guests had arrived. You could not have asked for a more surreally perfect wedding day. Except that it was time for the wedding to start—and Kris was nowhere to be found. I had no idea where he was. I called Roger—no answer. And of course we didn't have cell phones or even answering machines. In the meantime, Priscilla, my maid of honor, was also missing in action. I called down to her house and, once I got her on the phone, said as calmly as I could manage, "Priscilla . . . where are you?" And she said, "I just can't get my hair done—you're gonna have to start without me." I told her, "Well, that would be me starting without you—*and* my groom. I've got nobody up here but Mother and Daddy and a house full of guests." My

grandmother, Mama Stewart, who was now a hundred
and something years old, was in the back room at the
house, telling stories to try to keep people from leaving.
I said, "Priscilla, this is my wedding, I don't care what
your hair looks like. Please, please, *please* show up."

I was starting to give in to panic when Kris strolled in.
More like stumbled in. I don't know if he'd been drinking that morning but, having spent the night at Roger's,
he'd clearly had enough the night before to last him for
a couple of days. At that point somebody gave me half a
Valium because I was starting to get out of control because
I couldn't pull the pieces together and it was my wedding day. The wedding was really more for my parents
than anybody else. I really wanted things to be perfect—
not to mention on time—and to honor them and their
generosity in hosting the wedding in their home. And
in the end it finally did come together: Priscilla showed
up. We had the ceremony. There was a slight snafu with
the flower girl; she dutifully dropped the rose petals but
when I came down the aisle she suddenly pointed at me
and started screaming, "She's stepping on my roses!"
Afterward, there was cake and champagne along with
the usual minor catastrophes inevitable when you bring
two families, rock-and-roll musicians, and half of young
Hollywood to a house in the hills above Malibu.

To start with, both of my grandmothers were there:
Mama Stewart and Mama Coolidge, who had driven
from Ventura, just up the coast. These women had always

had a bit of a rivalry—they were pretty close in age and they were both very, very strong. Before she moved in with Mother and Daddy at Booker's ranch, Mama Stewart lived in the little house above the holler in Lafayette, where mother was raised. She was still in that house when, at age ninety-five, she developed cataracts, and at the time there was no cataract surgery for the elderly because going under general anesthesia at that age was considered too risky. So she was slowly going blind and there was nothing to be done. Then Mother and Aunt Phynis heard about a doctor in California who'd developed a procedure that dissolved cataracts without having to use general anesthesia. And so my grandmother, who had never been on an airplane and still called them "hill toppers"—and who had gone from Kentucky to Texas in a covered wagon when she was a girl and traded with the Indians and slept in the cornfields—boarded an airplane for the first time and flew to California. She had no fear. When she got to LA we were there to greet her. We asked, "Mama Stewart, how was your flight?" She said, "You know, I heard the hum of them engines and a song starts to come to me." She'd written a song on the plane. Everything was music to her.

And so Mama Stewart moved in with Mother and Daddy up at their house and had the surgery. When Priscilla and Booker got married, Mama Stewart was sitting in her little house in Tennessee and one of my aunts from Nashville, who was kind of the high-and-mighty oldest sister who thought that she was better than anybody else in the family, drove up all the way up to Lafayette in her Cadillac just to let Mama Stewart know that Priscilla had married a black man. She rolled into that house screeching, "Well, your precious Charlotte's child, Priscilla, that Priscilla's gone and married a black man." And Mama Stewart just looked at her and said, "The sin is in the heart, not in the skin." Her sister said, "You mean you don't care?" And Mama Stewart said, "No."

So Mama Stewart knew Booker was black but was already pretty much blind when she met him and so had never actually seen him. She wanted Booker to be there when she had the cataract surgery because Booker had this soft-spoken, velvety voice, and he and Mama Stewart would spend hours and hours talking. And so when her bandages were removed after the surgery, Booker's was the first face she saw. And she looked at him with tears in her eyes and she said, "When I see the face of Jesus Christ, he won't be more beautiful to me than you are." They had such a love affair. Booker called her his honeybee and wrote "Mama Stewart," a song about her: "Won't you sing me a song now and be my honeybee." Just so sweet. Kris also wrote her a song, with the refrain "Everything is beautiful in Mama Stewart's eyes."

Mama Stewart and Mama Coolidge managed to stay out of each other's way at the wedding, but Mama Stewart took the measure of Kris's mother, Mary, and apparently didn't like what she saw. Inside the house there were chairs set along the wall so people could sit and have wedding cake. I was finally starting to relax after the ceremony when I looked over and saw Mama Stewart slip a piece of cake onto the chair next to her just as Kris's mother came over to sit down. Now, Mary Kristofferson was as formidable a woman as Mama Stewart in her own way—remember, Kris always thought she would make an excellent five-star general. Of course Mary sat on the cake, and Mama Stewart, all sweetness and light, cooed, "Oh, ah'm so sorry, honey" in her Tennessee accent, which Mary wasn't buying for a minute. It was quite the fiasco. Mama Stewart was such a feisty little bugger. Near the end of the day, I noticed the party had thinned out and wondered where everyone had gone. I went down the hall and found Mama Stewart in her quarters with Sam Peckinpah and Larry Gatlin and James Coburn and all these Hollywood heavies sitting at her feet listening to her recite her true life poem and singing the stories.

I assumed that after the party Kris and I were going to stay in Malibu at a hotel or at Mother's. We hadn't really finalized those plans. Instead, we ended up at Roger's house. We'd just gotten married, it was ten o'clock on my wedding night, and Kris said, "We're just gonna stay here." I was so exhausted—also three months pregnant— that I didn't protest. I went to bed by myself and left Kris and Roger throwing 'em back and shooting pool. So: romance, romance.

Married life was, for the most part, a continuation of

our unmarried life: we both were working nonstop, still living in the moment. Kris was back on location and I was singing somewhere every night, it seemed, until one night at the Troubadour. By then I was gigging in jeans with the maternity stretchy panel and a burgundy turtleneck maternity top. As I stepped up on the stage to sing "Late Again," which Kris wrote and is a song I still perform ("I woke up late again this morning . . ."), it suddenly struck me that maybe it was time to stop performing. I'd reached a point in my pregnancy—and I assume this happens to a lot of other women—where I really didn't care about anything except having my baby. I wasn't concerned about what was happening beyond my pregnancy, or about what Kris did. I just told him, "You take care of solving the world's problems and keeping track of the big things. I'm going to leave that up to you because I'm having a baby."

Although we'd closed on the Malibu house weeks earlier, with the chaos of touring and Kris's movie schedule we'd never had time to move. By now it was late February. Casey was due March 4. Kris was gone again, and so one week before I was supposed to give birth, my sisters and friends and I packed up our things from the Garfield house in Hollywood and carted them out to Malibu. By this point I was pretty much living in these beautiful long white Mexican embroidered dresses. I felt like a Madonna. I was flat-out busy getting the house put together and the nursery ready. Kris finally came home, but not for long.

Our time was getting very short before he would have to leave for his next movie shoot. The March 4 due date was two weeks past—I had gained only twenty-one pounds during the pregnancy and I was now so late I was beginning to lose weight. I had to go to the doctor every day and get blood tests.

By now, Mother was staying at the house. Two days before Kris had to leave, I got up and, with still no signs of going into labor, decided to take action. I had heard that if you drank castor oil, you could actually induce labor. So I asked my OBGYN if it worked. He said you can drink all the castor oil you want—it will definitely speak to you, you'll know all about it. He made no claims about it hurrying along an overdue baby, but he'd heard the stories and said the fact that it goes through you so fast might have something to do with it supposedly working. But he wasn't promising anything.

So I got up that morning and drank an entire bottle of castor oil. And suddenly I was obsessed with roasting a huge turkey with dressing on the side and green beans. I started preparing this huge meal and Mother said, "Honey, what are you doin'?" And I said, "You know what? I'm having this baby. I'm having it. He's going to be here when this baby is born." While the meal was cooking, I went into the nursery. The crib was still in a box. So I put on my stretchy maternity jeans and my burgundy maternity turtleneck, got out a screwdriver, and single-handedly put the crib together because Kris hadn't. He wasn't really great with tools. (Oh, my God, at Christmas when we tried to assemble toys, he was impossible.) So I knew that I wasn't going to get much help from Kris. Besides, he was still asleep.

So I put the crib together, everything was sparkling clean, clean sheets on the bed, I had my bag packed, had the baby stuff ready to go. Mother just sat and watched and said, "Well, it looks like you may be nesting, honey. I think it might happen." After we finished my turkey dinner that night and I had done the dishes, I went into the living room, lay down on the floor with my knees up, and had my first cramp. Kris and I had done the Lamaze classes, so I started the breathing. During the night the cramping started to get a little bit more intense. I woke up Kris and told him, "I'm letting you know the baby is probably coming." He mumbled, "Well, wake me up when I need to take you in," and went back to sleep.

At six in the morning I woke Mother. We started timing the contractions and they were getting pretty close to five minutes apart. I got Kris out of bed and we drove straight to St. John's hospital in Santa Monica and checked in at nine a.m. I didn't know it at the time, but ten hours would pass before I was finally out of labor and held Casey in my arms for the first time. I spent most of the day huffing and puffing and pacing. Priscilla and Linda were there along with my best friends, Terri and Annie Rodgers, the twins from my early days in Hollywood. I was wearing the blue maternity robe that Terri had made that I'd worn throughout my pregnancy, which was fabulous because it had a drawstring so I could wear it after the baby was born, too. I still have it, for sentimental reasons. So there I was walking and doing my puffing and blowing and breathing when suddenly I felt a contraction that sent me to my knees. Priscilla looked at me and said, "Okay, now you're in labor." No kidding!

I went back into one of the labor rooms. There were seven women in delivery that day and I was the only one who didn't scream. The contractions just kept coming, all day long, but no baby. Kris was there and was helping, even though he had thrown up after watching a film at our childbirth class. Despite the pain, I didn't want drugs. I knew I was going to nurse and I didn't want drugs in my body. I finally ended up having a saddle block at the end because the baby had crowned and I wasn't dilated. After they gave me the epidural, Kris was holding my hand, but I could feel him start to get sick; I was sure he was going to pass out. I said, "Kris, stay with me, come on, stay with me."

And when Casey finally came it was a surprise because I had had three doctors tell me, without doing an ultrasound, that I was having a boy. They said, we hear the heartbeat as a boy's, you're carrying the baby like a boy, we're 90 percent sure it's a boy. But Priscilla said all along, "No, you're having a girl." She just knew. She kept bringing me dresses. So I had one little baby drawer that had all the Priscilla dresses in it, and thank God I had some girl clothes. When the doctor laid Casey on my belly, I said, "Is he okay?" and he said, "Look again, you've got a soprano." And I couldn't believe it. She was just so beautiful. She had this black hair, just like mine.

When Kris and I visited his mother before Casey was born, Mary started showing me all these pictures of her children. She said, "Look at all these blond children." She was a brunette. She said, "I never had anything to do with the way my children looked and you won't either." After Casey was born, Mary came to the hospital and brought a pair of little crocheted pants for Casey that were so cute. So of course I said, "Can I walk down to the nursery with you, Mary, to see the baby?" When we got to the nursery they had all the babies swaddled up in their cribs. Mary asked me, "Which one?" I said, "This one right here, the little brunette." And she looked at Casey and looked at me and just about-faced. Didn't say good-bye, "kiss my ass," or anything. Just walked out. Then I realized she was actually upset because I had had a child that looked like me. Mary had given me a bracelet when Kris and I were married that was made of coins that her husband had brought back from World War II. It was a beautiful bracelet and I wore it a lot. When Kris and I split up, the first phone call I got from Mary was, "Can you send the bracelet back?" I thought it might go to Casey, but okay. So I sent it back.

The year following Casey's birth in 1974 was the happiest time of my life. At first I stayed home in Malibu and nursed Casey while Kris continued his movie schedule—he costarred with Ellen Burstyn in Martin Scorsese's *Alice Doesn't Live Here Anymore* and played a biker in Peckinpah's *Bring Me the Head of Alfredo Garcia*. Kris loved having Casey in our lives, and for the moment we were a blissful family. Seven weeks after Casey was born, Kris and I embarked on a tour of Japan, Australia, and New Zealand and took her with us. Mother and Daddy came along and looked after Casey while we were performing. She was such a trouper. Babies are like little birds—they fall asleep when the sun goes down—so Casey handled the time changes much better than the jet-lagged adults. She also accompanied us on a European tour later in the year. Kris and I returned home from our travels with Casey and Mother and Daddy with what I felt was a renewed commitment to each other and to our new life as a real family. It seemed we had scarcely gotten settled back in Malibu before Kris was due in England to start filming the movie version of Yukio Mishima's *The Sailor Who Fell from Grace with the Sea* and had flown ahead. I flew over later with Casey and Terry Dupin, our road nanny. I had invited Terry to take the trip with me and to be my companion because Kris was filming all day and night and I didn't know anybody. Casey had a blanket—her "binky"—that she'd tickle her nose with when she was falling asleep. She couldn't go anywhere without that binky. She'd had it at the airport in LA, but then we got on the plane and there was no binky. And we had, what, a ten-hour ride ahead of us? I looked at Terry and said, "You know, we should probably start drinking right now, because this is going to be horrible." Luckily, Terry had a sweater that felt enough like Casey's binky, so when they turned out the lights on the flight she was fussy but didn't cry. And the second we landed, I called my old roommate Terri Rodgers. Her mother, Dorothy, knitted, and she had a picture of Casey's blanket. She said, "I'm gettin' Mom on it, it'll be there." So Dorothy knitted around the clock until the blanket was done and sent it as fast as anything could go, back then. Casey still has that, of course.

The studio had rented us this sea captain's house at the estuary in Cornwall. The sun didn't really come up until nine in the morning, and by four in the afternoon it was dark again. It was gloomy all the time. The best part of the day was walking with Casey in a pram in the morning drizzle to the bakery to get fresh scones and clotted cream. (Clotted cream actually comes from Cornwall, so that was pretty great.) But that was about it. It rained constantly, and there was nothing to do except watch the BBC (which went off the air at 3:30 in the afternoon) and wait for Kris to come back from the set.

Playboy had arranged to shoot a "pictorial," as the magazine euphemistically calls them, of Kris and Sarah Miles reenacting sex scenes from *Sailor* during the making of the movie. Both Kris and Sara were to be nude. They shot it at night after filming all day. Of course, I had no interest in going to that—not that I was invited. Now, Kris never drank wine, he pretty much drank hard liquor or beer. Apparently, they had only wine to drink during the *Playboy* shoot and, given the circumstances, he drank a lot. When he finally got home that night, Terry and I were at the table and Casey was in her high chair. Kris stumbled into the kitchen. He looked at me and then at Terry and said something rude to me and then something rude to Terry. I thought to myself, Oh, my God, this is bad. Kris was so, so out of it—I'd never seen him this far gone. Weaving down the hall, he would hit one wall and push himself off and hit the other side. I drew up behind him and tried to help. And suddenly he whirled around and struck me with his fist square in my eye.

Reeling from the pain, I realized I was more stunned than hurt. Kris was never, ever physically violent with me, no matter how viciously we fought. The closest he'd come was throwing a piece of lettuce, which went about two feet. We both had to laugh at that. But that night in Cornwall, he hit me, hard, in the face, and then stumbled down the hall to the bedroom. I cried for most of the night. When I got up the next morning with a shiner I confronted him. "Why am I here? Why would I want to be here? I'm here to be with you and to support you, I don't go to the set, I'm sitting in the house all day, it's dark, the TV is only on three hours a day." Kris was devastated, apologetic. He didn't remember any of it, not even the last part of the shoot or coming home. And I believed him. Of course, I had a black eye to remind him of what he'd done. And all of it—the blackout drinking, the violence—was coming from him feeling guilty about doing something that he knew was probably not the classiest thing, maybe just a little bit too much of an outlaw act, you know? That was the only time Kris struck me—it had never happened before, and it never happened again. But that was a really, really hard time.

Months later, when we were back home in Malibu, the phone rang. It was Mary. She said, "See what your precious Kris has done now." I said, "What?" She said, "Have you not seen *Playboy* magazine?" I told her no and asked someone to buy me a copy. On the cover were the words SARAH MILES AND KRIS KRISTOFFERSON IN THE SEXIEST STAR PICTORIAL EVER! My heart pounding, I opened the magazine, and all of the darkness of that time in the south of England came flooding back. There was Kris, nude, performing cunnilingus on Sarah, spread-eagled and also nude, her head thrown back in what looked like very real rapture. And much more of the same, page after page. Of course I had known the shoot was for *Playboy* but had no idea it would be so explicit. There was nothing aesthetically redeeming or particularly erotic about it—it was porn. I felt so betrayed and so embarrassed, my husband in these shots with Sarah Miles for all the world to see.

Kris was around but wasn't saying very much. I finally threw the magazine across the room, got dressed, and told him, "I'm going to work." I went into the studio that day; I was working on my next album, and I recorded Neil Sedaka's "The Hungry Years." It's such a beautiful song. "I miss the hungry years, the once upon a time, the lovely long ago . . ." That's what I chose to record. When I got to the studio I said, "I don't know what we've got up today but I do need to speak and I need to say what I'm feeling." So I recorded "The Hungry Years" and "I Don't Want to Talk About It." It was terribly sad. But if you listen to the record, it's all there. I was doing everything I could just to be able to get through those vocals. And I did it. There would have been no way to go in and do rock and roll, because my heart was breaking and that's what I needed to sing.

I had to live through the realization of not only what had happened in England but what was now being put before the whole world. This was my husband, after all. I had to weigh things and make a decision. It was something that had happened months earlier; we had a lot of life between the photo shoot and the magazine's publication, and that's what I had to look at. I had to think of Casey. Later, there was speculation—some of it by Kris, who said as much in an interview—that the *Playboy* pictorial was what broke our marriage apart. But the pictorial didn't break up our marriage. Nor did the night that he came back from the shoot and struck me. That was like getting attacked by Jim Gordon. Except Jim was out of his mind. Kris, in a drunken stupor born out of misguided guilt and rage, took a swing at the nearest target, which happened to be me. I'm not excusing it, justifying it, condoning or denying it. I'm just saying it was what it was. So I forgave him. And the next time I talked to Mary, when she called again, I said "You know what, Mary? If I could forgive him, surely you can. He's my husband. You're his mother."

And always, I just wanted to get back to Kris, no matter what was going on with us. We'd go through these horrendous wars and then as soon as we could just get some distance and separate, go back to our respective corners, we did manage to have a fabulous time when we came back together. But eventually the distances became greater, and the good times between us, more and more, became memories.

CHAPTER 9

Anytime...Anywhere

Kris had always been a drinker, but by the late seventies, with the pressures of stardom as both a singer-songwriter and an actor—*Pat Garrett* begat *Blume in Love, Alice Doesn't Live Here Anymore,* and *A Star is Born* in the space of three years—he was drinking heavily every day from morning to night. When he wasn't away filming or on the road, he lived in isolation in the back room of our house, where we'd installed a huge big-screen monitor before there were big-screen TVs. He would stumble out of the room first thing in the morning and start looking for vodka—he'd want me to make him what he called a Dirty Sock, which was grapefruit juice and vodka. And by the end of the day he would have been through a quart of vodka. He would roar from the back room, "*Riiittaa!*" And I would say, "Yes, what do you need? What can I do?" I was like a servant, constantly taking things back to him. I was complicit in creating that dynamic between us; I actively allowed it to happen, I admit that. I cooked the food, brought him the newspaper, whatever he wanted. I did all of the childcare. I went to the market one day and Casey was sleeping; I said, "I would have to wake her up to take her, could you just watch her?" And I came home and he was holding the baby's butt under the bathtub faucet because she needed a diaper change and he didn't know how to do it.

Pretty soon, my friends didn't come over because Kris would usually make them feel unwelcome. He raged at me a lot and then blamed the outburst—just like any of the bad behavior, whether it be the womanizing or emotional abuse—on the alcohol or, perversely, on me. And with every new incident I would feel my heart break a little bit more. My love would just wither under the anger and the yelling and the bullying and the sarcasm. I remember Priscilla and I wrote a song together. Kris came back from a trip and I played it for him and he actually said, "I wouldn't play that for anybody. You call that a song? That's a piece of shit." Well, it was the title song of *Satisfied*, my next album.

Movie stardom—something he'd never really sought— was overwhelming for Kris and helped fuel his drinking. Everybody wanted to touch him, everybody wanted to be with him. There was some part of him that obviously liked it or he wouldn't have done it, but I always knew that music was where his heart was, that he felt like he was kind of getting away with murder doing movies because he was not a trained actor. I think that he has since developed as an actor because he's done it for so many years, but at that time he was just playing himself in every movie. It was the same guy, in practically the same clothes. But after *A Star Is Born*, his fame exploded. And the movie fans were so much more aggressive and invasive than the music fans. I think that people who are famous for singing don't seem as accessible as movie stars. If you're listening to somebody on a record in your home, that's a whole different thing than going to a theater and seeing somebody on the screen, living their life and loving and having relationships and—in *A Star Is Born*—ultimately dying. We would be walking through an airport and Kris would have Casey on his shoulders, and these women would knock me aside and run up to him. And he would say, "I'm sorry, please, I have my baby, please." I think that was a big part of everything starting to fall apart. We had to hire security guards when we were on the road.

I love playing music, the energy you share with great players, and Kris was and is one of the greats, so playing with him was one of the joys of my life and a big part of our bond. But it started to get harder when Kris's drinking got out of control. I'm not an authority on alcoholism; I don't judge anybody. I just know what excess is. And his drinking had become so excessive that I would open the show and while I was doing my solo part, Kris would be backstage throwing 'em back. And that started to take away some of the joy for me because I never knew, when I went back out to do the duets, if he was even going to be able to stay on his feet. Some nights, he even started offering the audience their money back. He'd tell them, "If you didn't like this show, if I'm too fucked up, you can get your money back." Oh, my God, every time he did it, the promoters would be going nuts and our manager, Bert Block, would tell him, "No, don't do that, Kris, don't do that!" Then I'd have to go on stage and say, "Well, I know my husband has offered you your money back, but I'm not offering my half back because I'm very happy that you all are here and glad that we're here with you, he's just kidding." Try and get through that one. I'd tell Kris, "You know what? Give them your half back. I did fine. I'm doing my job. Just because you're not, you don't give back the money." And he would say, "But I mean it, I'll give 'em their money back because I think I was awful." And I'd tell him, "That's not why we're here. That's not how it works. That's not how any of this works."

Meanwhile, when Kris wasn't on location and we weren't on the road, our relationship continued to fray. Kris deluded himself into believing he was the victim, even though it was largely his behavior that created the problem between us. I had tried everything for us to have the same life and goals and purpose that we felt when we first met. Now we had none of that. I was crying all the time, because the marriage was broken and I couldn't fix it. I cried because I felt bad for Casey. I felt I wasn't a good mother and I certainly wasn't a good wife because good wives don't cry every day. I would say to Kris, "Please, please can we see a marriage counselor, can we see someone?" And he said, "Well, you see him, you're the one who's crazy." He was so unwilling to participate in saving the marriage. I knew I was reaching my limit. I kept telling him, "I can't live like this. I'm not going to live my life crying all the time, Kris. And once I walk out the door, then I don't come back. So if you want me not to leave, you have to help, you have to participate in the marriage. Because once I go out the door it's not debatable anymore. Once it's done, it's done."

Then, in a tremendous act of will, Kris suddenly stopped drinking. It was after he saw himself in *A Star Is Born* and watched his character, John Norman Howard, crash and burn as a result of alcohol. The shoot had been long and trying, and Kris had not gotten along with the director, Frank Pierson, a World War II veteran who criticized him for being in the army but not serving in Vietnam ("I was too drunk to give a shit," Kris said later). But seeing the movie was a real eye-opener for Kris. He said, "My God, I'm watching my future, my demise. This is what's going to happen to me." And he just stopped. The same way he'd stopped smoking: three packs of Bull Durhams a day to none. He had that kind of discipline— he'd made it through the elite US Army Ranger program in 1963, a brutal regimen where one's will to survive is challenged unrelentingly for three months. Once he was sober, he would wake up every morning and say, "I didn't know how bad I really felt till I stopped drinking." He started running a lot, but he was so much grumpier after he stopped drinking. Casey was a great source of joy for him during his transition to sobriety. He'd take her in the Jacuzzi or in the pool or just listen to music with her. He'd say, "Hey, Casey, put these headphones on, you're gonna love this." And they'd be in the living room, dancing—Casey just bouncing along with her daddy.

When you are sober, there are no rose-colored glasses and there's no medication. There is nothing that's going to tell you anything except the truth, and I think it was hard on Kris. He started to become jealous when I would go to the studio, because I was doing what he wanted to be doing, probably. I was recording *Anytime . . . Anywhere*, and while Kris was honoring our unspoken agreement that he'd stay out of the studio when I was working, I'd get to the house late at night to find that he had called David Anderle and asked him, "Where is she? What's going on? Have you got something going on with her?" And I'd have to reassure him, "No, Kris, we're working. I'm recording an album." I felt like I didn't have an inch of space around me to breathe when I got home. I was constantly being put in a position of having done something wrong, when in fact I was just making my music. And it got to the point that I would come home from the studio and I wouldn't even want to play any of it for him, because I didn't want him to taint this thing that brings me so much joy. Be happy for me, was what I wanted to say. And I think that deep down he was, but competing with that feeling was the fear that it was going to take me away from him.

I have always felt that in every relationship, for as long as it lasts, there is one person who is more in love than the other person at any given moment, and it shifts back and forth. The moments when that love is balanced are the magical times. That was when Kris and I would laugh our asses off and have the best time and love each other so very, very much. But then it would shift and we'd lose the harmony. The good times with Kris were so good that they almost transcended the bad. But the pain that the bad times inflicted on me still lives in my heart.

Casey was always able to bring us together as a family, although that's a big responsibility for a little kid. And we'd go visit Booker and Priscilla, Mother and Daddy, and Mama Stewart when they lived in Malibu, and that would help. But around this time, Priscilla and Booker bought 150 acres of redwood forest outside of Mendocino. Daddy built their house and then his and Mother's and Mama Stewart's, and they all moved up there. So now the family wasn't in Malibu anymore. We both felt like we'd had the rug pulled out from under us. Kris does well with family. I think that his greatest joy now is having all those kids and grandkids around him—it's the thing that makes him so happy. Of course, they'll all be there and he'll still take off and play golf. But just knowing that all the little chickens are back in the coop makes him happy.

And so it was with equal amounts of hope and trepidation that in 1977 I became pregnant with our second child. When I was eleven years old there were some Sundays at church that I took care of the nursery, and I would have five or six babies to take care of by myself. I had always loved babies and assumed that I would have multiple children. But as an adult I realized that that childhood dream didn't include being in the studio and going on the road and all the things that went along with that. Casey grew up on the road until she started school. She had her own bunk on the tour bus—"Casey's Cave," the sign above it read. But when she didn't travel with us, I can remember I would call home from, say, Australia, expecting for her to cry "Mommy, Mommy!" And I would get her on the phone and she would just say, if she would even talk to me, "Yeah, I'm fine. Whatever." I could tell that she missed me and that it was not easy for her. I feel horrible about that—I always did and always will. At some point a kid deserves a normal life, as normal as it can be. If I couldn't give that to her, I sure wasn't going to do it to another child. So I decided I should probably step off the road and do what I really wanted to do anyway, which was just to be pregnant. Kris and I had already named the baby Blake. Whether it was a boy or a girl—this was before sonograms, but I wouldn't have wanted to know in any case so I could be surprised—the baby would've been named Blake, because as Kris told me on the plane to Memphis all those years ago, he was a William Blake fanatic.

When I was seven months pregnant, we went to Hawaii and took Casey and, for once during those final, fraught years of our marriage, we had a great time. So I had hope that things might work out and we could stay a family.

One morning during the vacation, however, I realized that I couldn't feel the baby moving. I tried to reassure myself: I was healthy; I wasn't doing anything that would harm a child. I ate raw vegetables and had stopped smoking. When we got back to LA I went to straight to the obstetrician. After he examined me he called me into his office. He said, "You stopped smoking for this baby?" I nodded. He opened up a drawer and handed me a cigarette and said, "You're going to need this." Then he said, "The baby's heart is not beating. You're too far along for us to do anything right now, but you will miscarry." He told me they preferred not to do what's called a dilation and curettage unless it was absolutely necessary; it was safer for me to miscarry the baby. So I had to wait. But what happens in this situation is that if you don't miscarry naturally, the baby will start to dissolve back into the placenta. It's called a missed abortion and it's fairly rare. At that point they would have to remove the fetus because it could lead to major infection—it would have killed someone from my grandmother's generation. But they wanted to wait and see if I would miscarry because that was the safest option.

A month went by and at first I stayed home, but pretty soon I couldn't stand it so I started going to the market in Malibu. I was still visibly pregnant, so of course people would ask, "How's the baby?" I tried to finesse the question but after a while I just couldn't. So I'd answer, "The baby is dead." It was the darkest, darkest time in my life because there was not really anything that I could do. And it was so uncomfortable—nobody knew how to deal with it. I never miscarried, and they finally had to do the procedure. I never knew but I'll always believe it was a boy. A week afterward, I woke up to find that I had started hemorrhaging. I called Priscilla—Kris was away—and she raced me to the hospital. She had on some kind of one-piece jumpsuit, and the elastic on the top was loose. At the hospital, when she was running down the hall to get me into surgery, of course her top fell off. My doctor said, "My God, Priscilla, can you not let her have this moment? Can you not see that your sister needs to be the center of attention?" It was great to be able to laugh in middle of that.

After I recovered we all went to Albuquerque, where Kris was filming *Convoy*. Priscilla and Linda came, too. It was good to have my sisters close after everything I'd been through. Ali MacGraw was Kris's costar in the movie. Ali and I were not friends at the time, although we later became best friends—a first among Kris's leading ladies. I remember Ali sitting at one end of the swimming pool with some other women one day while Priscilla and Linda and I were at the other end. And Ali looked at us and yelled, "Hey you! Cherokee mafia!" Barbara Carroll, the jazz pianist who was married to our manager, Bert Block, was there, too. And to fill our days Barbara and I took tap dancing lessons, of all things. There was a prima ballerina there and Linda was studying ballet with her. It was such a palliative to spend a few weeks like that, although I was still grieving the loss of my unborn child and would for some time.

It wasn't long after I'd returned from New Mexico that I'd found myself in the kitchen doing the dishes when my version of "Higher" came on the radio. And almost before I could dry my hands I was plunged into the frenzy of having a song and an album turning into worldwide hits. "Higher" was all over the radio during the summer of '77, all over the world. My label, A&M, kept peeling singles off *Anytime . . . Anywhere.* When David Anderle and I had been picking songs for the album, Jerry Moss had called me into his office and played me Boz Scaggs's "We're All Alone," the song that closed his career-making 1976 album *Silk Degrees.* Jerry pointed out that the song was already in a million homes and was perfect for a woman singer to cover. I'd agreed and added it. When A&M released it as the album's second single, "We're All

Alone" became almost as big a hit as "Higher," peaking at number 7, followed by my cover of the Miracles' "The Way You Do the Things You Do," which hit number 20. Meanwhile, *Anytime . . . Anywhere* hit number 6 on the album charts and was certified platinum. The varied styles of the songs on the album expanded my audience to fans of R&B and what would later be called adult contemporary. It was such a fun, eclectic album—I covered Kris's "Who's to Bless and Who's to Blame," even the Bee Gees' "Words," which Priscilla and I used to sing at the Whirlaway Club in our gold and silver lamé dresses when we lived in Memphis.

Among its other gifts, *Anytime . . . Anywhere* was for me a great distraction. It came along a month after I lost the baby and helped me through the grieving and allowed me to let go because, really, there was nothing I could do. My doctor told me, "Physically you're healthy. You could get pregnant again. Emotionally you need to wait a year. Psychologically this is probably not the best time for you to get pregnant again." Which was good to hear, because I had to go on the road for the rest of the year to support the album. And, in truth, after I lost our second child I lost those dreams about a big family, too. Now that my career started to take off I felt like I needed to give it whatever energy I had.

Performing while I was still grieving the loss of that child was a challenge. But as I've mentioned, taking any kind of problems on stage is never an option. It's like walking on stage wearing no clothes and thinking that nobody's going to notice. When Mother passed on August 15, in 2012, I had a gig on the eighteenth and I knew she wouldn't want me to not do that gig. So I cried right up to the minute I had to get my makeup on, did the show, walked off stage, and fell apart again. I didn't say my mother died two days ago—you don't do that to an audience. If you're not going be able to get through it, then don't do it. People don't pay money to come hear about your problems. Connie Nelson used to say, "If you haven't had enough sleep, and you've been up half the night, if you don't tell anybody, they don't know." Exactly.

So I soldiered through the tours for *Anywhere . . . Anytime* that took me around the world, and in the process began to come to peace with myself and what had happened. I felt something change in me. I was a little more outgoing. I started wearing different kinds of clothes, things that were more colorful, beautiful fabrics. It was a transformation that I didn't really understand but allowed myself to embrace. But it puzzled me. I decided to have a reading with a psychic. She took my hand in hers, studied it, and said, "There has been a 'walk-in' in your life." I asked her what that was. She said, "It's when a soul merges with yours. Has anything happened?" I told her about the car accident when I was thirteen and she said that no, it would be something else. "What about pregnancies?" I told her about losing the baby, and she said, "That's probably when it happened." The psychic said that the soul of my unborn child had merged with mine. She said, "That child is still a part of you."

Forty years later, it still is.

CHAPTER 10

Leaving While You're Still in Love, and Other Assorted Revelations

Kris and I went on the road together after *Anytime . . . Anywhere* was released, but it was different from our past shows because I had been validated as a solo artist on such a massive scale. Despite being accepted by so many people, I still wanted Kris's approval. And I was still so connected to Kris that people couldn't say Rita without saying Kris. And that followed me around for so very long. I mean, now I'll talk to people and I'll say I was married to Kris Kristofferson and they'll go, "Really? You mean that guy in *Blade*?"

In the years leading up to the final split, I kept pressing Kris to go to counseling with me. When he stopped drinking I hoped that some of his emotionally abusive behavior might diminish, and it did somewhat. But the dynamic between us had already been established, and that doesn't change overnight. We needed the help of therapy, somebody impartial to sit down and look at both people and ask the hard questions. In my case: "Why are you an enabler? Why do you take care of him like he's a child? Why do you let him do this?" But Kris steadfastly refused to go to therapy and our problems worsened.

At that moment so many doors had opened for me. I had my own money and I had a record company that was 100 percent in my corner. Kris didn't have that, and it was beginning to color his attitude toward my work—even when I was covering one of his songs. When I recorded "Late Again," I changed a note or two of his melody. When I played it for him, he said, "If anybody else butchered my melody like you just did, I'd tell them to go fuck themselves." George Jones could sing Kris's songs all over the place but I wasn't supposed to. It was strange; I just never got it. But I was tiring of him trying to wear down my confidence. The worst part of it was dealing with the womanizing. Every time Kris left town and went on the road he behaved as if we had an understanding that he was allowed to do whatever he wanted.

By 1979, when I finally confronted Kris during the filming of *Heaven's Gate*, I didn't feel like I fit into his life anymore. He had had plenty of time to act, had he cared. I will never know why he didn't see that the marriage was failing, or that I meant what I said about once I go through the door. But once I left, it was unbelievable how Kris pursued me. He was in town all the time—can we go to the movies, can we please talk, can we do this, can we do that. He begged and pleaded for me to come back, promised how it would be different. He wanted to see a marriage counselor. And I wouldn't, because that door was truly closed. Also, I was, and am, incredibly stubborn. I had made my decision. I don't think that people really change, honestly, or at least they can't change very much. I had a strong sense that if I went back and tried to make it work that I would find myself in the same place again. And at that point—I'd seen it happen with so many women—it's harder to walk out that door again, it's harder to make that break. And it's really hard on the children.

When Kris and I split, I took what was mine and left. I was served the divorce papers on Christmas Eve. There was not a big battle. We agreed to joint custody of Casey. We never went to court; we just settled. For the first time, there was nothing to fight about. Despite the fact that I had found our home in Malibu, Kris kept the house because I had signed a prenup that said he got to keep it if we divorced. I didn't remember that, but apparently his business managers had me sign something to that effect before we got married. We jointly owned twenty-six acres in Hana, Maui, and agreed as part of the divorce that whoever built first on the land, the other would sell them their share. (I later sold my half to Kris when he and Lisa, his beautiful wife of the past thirty-five years, built a home there.)

When I heard that Marc Anthony and Jennifer Lopez were splitting up, I think I actually had tears in my eyes.

And for the first time I understood what our fans experienced when Kris and I divorced. People, to a certain extent, live vicariously through the lives of celebrities they admire. So when Kris and I split, there was a great grieving among our fans; people seemed to feel like they had to choose sides. The irony is that in spite of his bad behavior and bad faith, the fact that I had done the leaving allowed Kris to be portrayed—and to portray himself—as the aggrieved party, and me as the heartless wretch who had abandoned him and Casey.

A year after the divorce I was stunned to see Kris and Casey smiling out from the cover of *People* magazine. To read the story—a typically unctuous *People* profile lauding Kris—you'd think that I had deserted my family. There were pictures of Kris and Casey on the cover, Kris and Casey inside. I wasn't interviewed or even told the story was coming. Regarding his "recovery" from our breakup, Kris was quoted: "I thought the marriage would last forever, but there was a competition there I wasn't aware of. I guess the pressures of keeping two artists not only under the same roof but also on the same stage are greater than I thought. There are some things you just can't make work." This was such a blatant distortion of reality that I didn't know whether to laugh or cry. But the story's implication that I had abandoned my husband and daughter, when I had spent years desperately trying to keep us together, was almost too much to bear. That story still hurts me to this day.

To keep Casey's life as stable as possible after the divorce, we made sure to book our tours and Kris's movie shoots so that somebody was always at home with her. When we both were in town she'd divide her time pretty much equally between my place in Hollywood and Malibu. It wasn't long before I heard that there were endless women passing through the house. When Casey stayed with me, I never said anything bad about Kris. But apparently when I was not around the talk about me was so bad that I was a joke at the house at Malibu. This was before Kris settled down with Lisa. But at that time, the only way Kris could reconcile my leaving was to make a joke out it—that there must be something wrong with me to have left him.

I still don't know the damage the divorce may have done to Casey. She didn't want to talk about it when she was little and we don't talk about it now. She does understand it as an adult, but I think that it hurt her as a child. She is a wife and a mother herself now, so she sees things differently. But at the time she was just a little kid and had to listen to people talk shit about me all the time. It must have been incredibly confusing for her.

One night I found Casey in her bedroom at my house, packing her little bag. And I said, "Casey, honey, what are you doing? We're not going anywhere." She said, "Well, I called my dad and he's going to pick me up." And I said, "Why?" She said, "Because I want to go back to Malibu." Kris came and picked her up that night. And by the time they left my heart was breaking but . . . you've got to behave like an adult. I couldn't get mad at Casey and go storming out of the house yelling; she was just a little kid trying to deal with everything. And the Malibu house was where she had grown up. So I understood that she was comfortable there; also, Kris was buying her ponies and anything she wanted. That was his way of being a daddy because he didn't have a lot of training. And he did become a better dad and a more proactive father.

When Kris and I first met on our flight to Memphis, he'd told me about his two children, Tracy and Kristo. I think Tracy was maybe five and Kristo about a year old. And he hadn't seen those kids in months. I'm sure he financially supported them, but he wasn't helping Fran, his former wife, or going to see them. When I entered the picture, I started having the kids come and visit us for the weekend, or we would go to see them. Because I was thinking, *There are two kids involved in this, not just Kris and me. There are two children who need their daddy.* Tracy told me later, "When you came into the picture, you gave us back our dad because you started involving us." And it was gratifying to see that Kris, when he put in the effort, could be the father that his children deserved.

Although I missed collaborating with Kris after the divorce, it was liberating to control my professional life without having to consider his. I was touring completely on my own now, with a band devoted exclusively to my music (though I continued to play some of Kris's songs). I'm a pretty tolerant bandleader, so long as the show goes off the best it can. I don't tolerate willful unprofessionalism. I like a loose, cooperative atmosphere with the musicians who play with me—but make no mistake, you'd better hit the stage on time and be ready to roll. The guys could do what they wanted when we were done working—I didn't, and don't, care what they did offstage or out of the studio. But you've got to come to the stage sober and you've got to do your job. That's just always been a rule. Carmen Grillo, the former Tower of Power guitarist who's with Sons of Champlin now, played in my band for several years and later told me, "The thing that I remember is that you were the best boss I ever had because if it weren't for you I would've spun out of control. You kept me walking that straight line until I realized that that was the only way to walk. You were like the mama bear; you kept everybody in line till the show was over."

I take what I do seriously and I'm not at all conflicted about busting anybody—I don't care who they are—who's not with the program 100 percent. Before he died of a heart attack in 1992, Jeff Porcaro was LA's number one session drummer, filling the void left by Jim Gordon after he succumbed to his schizophrenia and murdered his mother. Jeff played in Steely Dan for years and was the drummer for hire on dozens of the biggest albums in the seventies and eighties, from Boz Scaggs's *Silk Degrees* to Don Henley's *The End of the Innocence*. He founded Toto with three other LA session players. He was at the top of his game when I hired him to play on one of my albums. We'd just done a run-through of a track when I heard him tell the engineer, "Take Rita out of my headphones." I feel the vocal is an instrument as much as those of the other players; we all play together. So I waited a beat or two and said over the studio intercom, "Jeff? This is Rita. Can you hear me okay?" He said he could. I said, "Good. Jeff, don't bother coming to the studio tomorrow."

I toured the world several times over after *Anytime . . . Anywhere*, the hardest and longest stretch of work I've done before or since. And though I took care of myself as best I could, the strain of overwork was beginning to affect my most precious asset: my voice. I started noticing that I seemed to have only half my voice on some shows, but I had to keep going because we had all these dates booked into what seemed like eternity. It got so bad that many times a doctor would come to the hotel the afternoon before a show and give me an injection to take down the inflammation of my vocal cords. But you can't do that all the time. I would do that if we were playing ten-thousand-seaters, but if I was playing a club, I didn't really want to have an injection to get through an hour-and-a-half gig.

As soon as I came off the road I saw Joe Sugarman, a doctor in Beverly Hills who's known as the singers' doctor, and he discovered that I had developed nodules on my vocal cords. With plenty of trepidation I had the surgery to remove them, and was so relieved when it was a complete success. I also worked with Lillian Glass, a speech specialist. Lillian told me that because of the way Southerners speak, I had developed a habit of, as she put it, "frying" my words—speaking them with the sort of flat affect and lower register you hear in Gwyneth Paltrow's voice—which, if you're a singer who's already having vocal problems, can get you in real trouble. So I worked with Lillian and she taught me a lot. When I became one of VH-1's first VJs, she helped me to learn to modulate my speaking voice—I'd never done that sort of speaking before, and had ended up sounding a bit monotonous. Lillian, bless her, fixed that, too. It's crazy, sometimes, what we have to learn in this life.

I was talking to Quincy Jones three years after *Anytime . . . Anywhere* about the effort on A&M's part to have another hit. I'd had singles since then that had performed well but not another album that charted like that. And Quincy said, "Rita, it's a big circle. The pendulum swings down, the pendulum swings back up. Just have faith. It'll be back up there." I was at one of those gala things in New York City, a charity ball with Dionne Warwick and

Frank Sinatra and Liza Minnelli. As luck would have it, I was seated next to Sammy Davis Jr. He was asking me what was going on and I said, "I'm just trying to figure out what I'm going to do on my next record." He said, "Record? What do you need a record for?" I said, "Well, that's what I do, I make records." He said, "Actually, no, what you do is you sing, and because you sing you make records. If you're waiting for your record to take you to the next step in your life, maybe it's time for you to stop making records for a minute and learn how to do your craft. Learn how to be a singer, learn how to be an entertainer, be a performer if that's what you want to do, but don't let the records drive you."

And it was like right between my eyes—unbelievable, the impact that that had on me. I did exactly what he said and I really started paying attention to what I was doing and started putting together my shows more conceptually, thinking more about communicating with the audience and looking at people and speaking from my heart. I still do it. I'm always telling a story that my band has never heard before. For the past ten years my drummer, Lynn Coulter, has been saying, "You've got to write this shit down. You have got to write a book." Well, Lynn, here's your book. Hope you've enjoyed it. I know I have.

I've always had tremendous respect and gratitude for my fans—they've been with me for decades and I've become great friends with some. I would do anything in the world for them. And I learned an important lesson about the bond between us. After singing "Higher" every night for two decades, I decided I was going to stop playing it live—I was just going to take it out of the show. When I told a friend of mine, Nick Chavez, who is now a famous Beverly Hills hairdresser, his response was unequivocal: "You can't do that, Rita. That's what they come to hear." I said, "No, if they're coming to hear me sing, they're going to be happy with whatever I choose."

That night, Nick and I went to see Luther Vandross at the Hollywood Bowl. Now, Luther was my favorite male singer, ever. There is something about the tone and the timbre of Luther's voice that wraps around my heart. I get lost in his voice and in his interpretation of a song; the way he can make a note cry breaks my heart and penetrates every fiber of my being. Luther had just released a new record. And at the Hollywood Bowl that night he came out and performed only the new album. He didn't do any of his older songs. And when the show was over I told Nick, "I am so unfulfilled. Did you know he was going to do that?" He said, "No, I wouldn't have come." I told him, "I so get what you were saying about not playing 'Higher.' Thank you."

Here's the thing: You have to sing it like it's the first time, every time. Because there are people out there and for them, this is the first time they've heard it live. So yes, I still sing—and love singing—"Higher." It's my finale to this day.

At some point I really did realize that life is more of a spiritual journey than anything. That is the most important thing to me, and much more important than having hit records is my spiritual growth and my path and trying to stay on it and be a good person. It's all about the journey. Sometimes the path is surrounded by rainbows, and sometimes it's buried in the mud. As long as you don't start believing your own PR and remember who you are and where you came from—which is pretty easy to do because you put your pants on one leg at a time just like everybody else—you'll be fine. That's the way it's always been for me. I'm still here and I still have a lot of gratitude for the whole process of being able to make music.

Somebody asked me recently if I was going to retire. Well, I'm never going to retire. Maybe I'll leave the music business, but I'll never stop being a singer. I don't know how long people are going to want to look at me, but I hope they'll always want to hear me sing. I get tickled to death hearing my songs whenever, wherever. I was in Marshalls with a girlfriend and they were playing my recording of "All Time High," the theme for *Octopussy*, the James Bond film. When they cut into it to make an announcement on the PA, I started singing right where it left off. My girlfriend turned her cart around and ran the other way—"I don't know you! I don't know you!"

When I wake up in the morning the first thing that I think is, I can sing. God gave me a gift. There is nothing like the power of music. I learned that firsthand from

Daddy's preaching. When he'd do the invitation at the end of the sermon, they always played the saddest song: "Just as I am without one . . ." And the congregation would think, Oh . . . I need to go rededicate my life to Jesus! But you know that some people didn't walk down that aisle for any other reason except that the music made them cry.

I was driving my old green Volkswagen in Memphis the first time I heard Aretha Franklin sing "A Change Is Gonna Come." When that song came on the radio and Aretha sang in that molasses voice of hers, "And I was born by the river . . . ," tears shot out of my eyes. I pulled the car over and just wept. When music can convey that kind of power, there is nothing like it. Music is better than a good meal, it's better than sex, it's better than anything. It just rules.

And so every morning of every day, I give thanks. Thank you, God. Thank you. I can sing.

Epilogue

For all of our lives, Priscilla and I talked at least two or three times a week. We were very, very close. We did everything together. We took care of Mother and Daddy together when they were older. Starting in 1997 we performed together—along with her daughter, Laura Satterfield—as Walela (Cherokee for hummingbird), singing Native American themed songs that we wrote together—we performed at the opening ceremonies for the 2002 Winter Olympics in Utah. We'd been inseparable since we were little, when Priscilla told me she'd been waiting for me to be born.

Priscilla and Booker had split at the same time I left Kris. (Priscilla, Linda, and I had, unbeknown to one another, left our husbands on the same day—Mother called me and said, "I don't know what's going on with you all, but Kris just called and said I gave birth to black widow spiders—what's he talking about?") I had had enough success that I was able to be financially independent and for a while Priscilla was, too. She ended up moving to New York and marrying Ed Bradley, the *60 Minutes* correspondent, in 1981. After she and Ed divorced and she came back to California three years later, it was hard for her to get back into the music business, and she never really fully did. She had recorded two beautiful solo albums, *Flying* and *Gypsy Queen*, and made several more albums with Booker. And she was supportive of her children's artistic endeavors, as Mother and Daddy had been with us—her son Paul Satterfield went on to have a big career as an actor on television (*General Hospital*) and in the movies, and Laura, who had her own singing and songwriting career in addition to performing in Walela.

Priscilla was living with me in West Hollywood when I sold my house and moved to Fallbrook, near San Diego. When I put my house on the market, Priscilla started weighing her options. Priscilla, of all people, was not some Blanche DuBois. Then she met this guy through my real estate agent. He was of Lakota Sioux and French descent and lived in Seattle and was vaguely involved in various real estate deals, although it was never really clear to me what, exactly, he did. Priscilla moved to Washington with him—they later were married in Mendecino by Daddy—and moved back to California to Thousand

Oaks, north of Los Angeles, where they lived for the next seventeen years.

She was at the house in Thousand Oaks when I called her on October 1, 2014, to wish her happy birthday. She'd just turned seventy-three. Things weren't going well. Her husband—I refuse to name him—was always on the edge of a deal that was just about to come through but never did. That was the last time we spoke. The next day, Laura discovered her body in the bedroom, called the police, and then called me. Some time after we'd spoken on her birthday, her husband killed my beautiful, brave Priscilla with a hand gun and then—as it is inevitably phrased in newspaper accounts of murder-suicides—turned the weapon on himself.

I was home alone when I got the news—my husband, Tatsuya, was up in Irvine for the day. I called Linda and my brother, Dick, and Casey; then I called my old friends Lou Moller and Sandy Hull. Sandy came right over (she thought I was calling about my ailing nineteen-year-old cat that actually died two days later). Lou was on the next plane from New York. I called Connie Nelson— dear Connie, from the days when Kris and Willie were on the loose and we thought our marriages to our famous husbands would last forever—and she flew in from Austin. The news spread quickly through the musicians' network and the condolences started pouring in. I received a beautiful email from Graham; I was in a state of shock and confusion from the suddenness of it all, and those simple gestures of kindness made it possible for me to handle the awful logistics of the next few days and weeks. Thankfully, Priscilla's death didn't get much play in the media. The way her life ended was so ghastly and at odds with the way it should have been that I couldn't bear the thought of her remembered for being murdered.

We held a memorial for Priscilla on a brilliant Saturday in November at the Self-Realization Fellowship's Lake Shrine temple in Pacific Palisades. It was the perfect, peaceful antidote to the brutality of her death, and the service unfolded like a prayer, with the gentlest of rhythms, as we sang and remembered and blessed the passing of my beautiful, beautiful Prissy. Her children Paul, Laura, and Lonnie all spoke from their hearts about the great love that they held for their mother. So many people had reached out to me in the weeks leading up to the service. Kris was devastated. When Casey gave him the news, he told her that after I had left him, he answered the phone one day at the house in Malibu. It was Priscilla. She said, all innocence, "Can I speak with Rita?" Kris told her, "Rita's not here. She left me." And Priscilla waited just long enough and purred, "That's *righhhhhhhhtt. . . .*" David and Stephen, bless them, sent flowers to the memorial. And the fact that Graham attended meant the universe to me. He'd responded to my invitation saying that he was sorry but that he would be on the road that day—he lives in Hawaii now. Then, three days before the service, he emailed that he had rearranged his schedule and would be there. And he was. Dear Graham, how fortunate I am to know you—the generosity of your spirit lifts me to this day.

I was still grieving for Priscilla the week before Christmas when a black box containing the ashes of her husband arrived in the mail. He was not loved by his family, who wanted nothing to do with his remains, so I had arranged to have his body cremated—I know that's what Priscilla would have wanted. I buried them in the avocado groves that border my property and mostly forgot about them until I woke up on New Year's Eve and said, "The new year cannot come in with these ashes in my life." So at seven in the morning I went out to the groves, dug up the box, and put it in my car.

I started driving out past Temecula, the back way to Palm Springs if you know the roads, deep into the California desert. When I came upon a two-lane blacktop that cut across the highway and seemed to disappear into infinity, I said to myself, I think I'll go over there. So I went down that road a little way and came to a wide dirt road that wound up the side of a hill. As I started up this road I kept saying to myself, There'll be a sign, there'll be a sign, I know there will be a sign. And then I saw it—an actual sign off to the right that said: TRESPASSERS WILL BE SHOT ON SIGHT. And I said to myself, I think I found my sign.

I turned the car around so that if anybody came out with a gun I could get away, then got out of the car, walked beyond the sign, and found a place. I opened the box and shook out the ashes. They didn't poetically waft away in the wind—they just fell from the box and lay there on the dead desert floor. So that was that. It was silent except for a cutting wind that rustled the chaparral and worried my hair. I looked to the sky and the setting sun, got in my car, and drove off. I scrubbed my hands in a truck-stop ladies' room and drove straight to Temecula and did some retail therapy. Yes, I went shopping—oh my God, how Prissy would have wanted me to shop after that. We loved shopping, from the time we were little girls to our first days in Hollywood when we would spend two hours in a drugstore with ten dollars between us and have so much fun.

Priscilla was my best friend—and I still just feel robbed. As I said at her memorial, "Good-bye, Priscilla June. Gone too soon. Gone too soon."

If I kept in touch with everyone I've known in my life, I wouldn't have time to sleep. Connie Nelson is the go-to person for that because she somehow has the time and keeps all of us connected.

Despite our divorce, Kris and I have kept our relationship alive and loving, and we remain very good friends. Kris and I talk about our lives, we talk about our children, and we talk about our music. Something I've observed about Kris is that people who are nice and loving when they are younger become sweet elders, whereas people who are not nice become mean old people. Despite our differences when we were married, Kris remains one of the sweetest men I've known. He's precious—precious with his wife, with all of his children, and with me.

Graham Nash is one of the best guys I've met in my life. He's the loveliest man and a great songwriter. He's written some songs I'm going to record on an upcoming album, and the fact that he wants me to record them makes me incredibly happy.

After not seeing each other for more than ten years, Leon and I played a tribute to Joe Cocker at the 2015 Lockn' Festival in Virginia. The organizers had originally planned to reunite the surviving members of the Mad Dogs & Englishmen band and Joe had agreed to appear, but, tragically, he died on December 22, 2014, at his home in Colorado after battling lung cancer. He was seventy. I was on Bonnie Bramlett's Facebook page when I heard he'd passed. Joe was true to himself and his music and he didn't follow, didn't emulate, didn't imitate—he was just who he was. We became quite close for a while following the Mad Dogs tour, when he was so broke and broken down and I'd taken him over to Prissy's and Booker's to recuperate. I was delighted that the reunion concert went on after his death—I know Joe would have loved that, he was the consummate trouper. With the Tedeschi Trucks Band serving as host band, veterans of the Mad Dogs tour, including Leon on piano; Bobby Jones,

Claudia Lennear, Pamela Polland, Matthew Moore, and Daniel Moore and myself on vocals; Joe's original pianist Chris Stainton on keyboards, and Chuck Blackwell and Bobby Torres on percussion, performed a suite of songs from the tour. I sang lead on "Superstar," my old solo spot, and on "Bird on a Wire." It was a great reunion and night, and a thrill to sing onstage again with Leon, who along with Delaney and Bonnie opened the door to my career and so much more when they encouraged me to leave Memphis for Los Angeles.

My parents both passed in 2012—Daddy died, of leukemia, on February 29. Mother came to live with me in May that year and passed after a third, massive stroke on August 15. They were married seventy-four years. They say that the love between some people is so profound and deep that when one partner dies, part of the other partner dies with them. Mother was indomitable and had tremendous courage, and when Daddy died—although she missed him terribly—she didn't succumb to self-pity. I was talking to Priscilla on the second anniversary of Mother's passing and she told me, "I remember Mother leaving to go and live with you, and as she walked to the car, she turned and looked over her shoulder and she looked at me, she looked at the house and smiled, and got in the car and left. She didn't make a big deal out of it. She was brave."

On Mother's sixtieth birthday we were on the road and I asked her, "How does it feel to be sixty?" She said,

"I feel like I did when I was twelve." I thought, Oh, that's so cute, but now I totally understand. As you get older, you gather layers and layers and layers of life. And you learn to wear them and carry them proudly, or you let them take you down.

And I choose to wear mine.

Acknowledgments

I dreamed of someday writing a book when I learned to read at four years old. It is with gratitude that I acknowledge the many players who brought this dream to fruition.

To Nelly Neben: I have never had a more creative and determined business partner than you, my friend and manager. You pushed me out of my comfort zone and proved that anything is possible. You had the vision, you persevered and doors opened. You made this book happen. Thank you, Nelly and Axis Management.

To Daniel Greenberg, my literary agent: Thank you for believing in me and this project and big thanks for putting me together with Michael Walker.

To Michael Walker: Your patience throughout the months that turned to years would be miraculous were it not for your brilliance as a music journalist and published author. Thank you, not only for the countless hours of listening, but for hearing me. You inspire me.

To my editor Jennifer Barth: From the beginning, you simply asked that I tell my story with truth and honesty. You helped me stay the course and I thank you. You're the best.

To my publisher HarperCollins: Thank you for embracing my story and welcoming me into the fold.

To Tim Goodwin: Thank you for always being there for me with wisdom and humor.

To Diane Sutton: You make me laugh even through the tragic times, always sensible and generous of heart.

To Brenda Lee: You will always be the one and only Little Miss Dynamite and I love you girl.

To Don Nix: The King of Cool, thank you for sharing and showing me around the Memphis music scene.

To Leon Russell: The reigning "Master of Time and Space." Your talent is a river of beauty than runs deep and wide, and I am blessed to know you.

To Bonnie Bramlett: It would take another book to say all the things and ways I love your face, your soul, your gift, and your laughter. Our journey is still unfolding and everlasting.

To Joe Cocker: Rest in Peace, Gentle Superstar. You live in the heart of the world.

To David Anderle: You were a quintessential artist who effortlessly found the balance in color, sound, instruments, songs, and players. The music world misses you and thanks you.

To Jerry Moss and Herb Alpert: Thank you for trusting and believing in me at a time when artists were truly given a safe home at A&M Records, the family label.

To Bob Jenkins: RIP. Thank you for following me with your camera and documenting 1970s LA.

To Linda Wolf: Thank you for your passion to keep Joe Cocker and the Mad Dogs and Englishman still front and center.

To Terri and Annie Rodgers and the Teenage Bad Girls: We haven't changed much, thanks for that.

To Mary Stuart Simpson Orbe: Thank you for our lifetime of unconditional love for each other, our children and the FSU Noles.

To Connie Nelson: My foreverlasting best friend who will always keep me connected, young, and laughing long after we've crossed over. You know me better than I know myself!

To Graham Nash: You changed my life by simply sharing your love and friendship that is as warm and present as the day we met. Thank you.

To Stephen Stills: I probably don't need to ask but please never lose that delightful, mischievous spirit that keeps you so young, like Peter Pan.

To David Crosby: You truly are one of the good guys who keeps getting better all the time. Thank you.

To Eric Clapton: I was and will always be in awe of

your talent. You have become a role model for all singers and musicians. You rock and you roll.

I want to thank my band: JT, John, Lynn, Randy, Mary, Lynn, and Gregg, for all the continuing great times playing music. I'm lost without you.

To the fans: A huge thanks. You are the reason I'm still here.

To Kris Kristofferson: Thank you for giving so much of yourself to the family, inspiring singer-songwriters, and to the Heart and Soul of America. You are a national treasure for us all.

To Lisa Kristofferson: Your strength and commitment to your family is like few women I've known. You shine through in each of your children and in Kris.

To my book club, "Reading Between the Wines": Thank you all for not only being the greatest girlfriends, but a loyal support system for many years, past, and many to come. To our Queen, Mrs. Logan, and ladies, I hope you like the book.

To the Fallbrook Downtown Dolls—Sandy, Tami, Leila, Tammi, Terri, and Dianna: You are my tribe and my posse. I love you all.

To Dick, my brother, who is always by my side when I reach out: You've always been the oldest, the smartest, and your walk, your talk, like Daddy.

To Linda Lou, my precious sister, devout Christian, singer, and leader: You're the best cook in the family. You will walk in beauty.

ACKNOWLEDGMENTS

To Casey, my beautiful daughter—mother, wife, friend, and teacher. You are my finest moment. From the first time I saw eternity in your newborn eyes, I was humbled by the miracle of love. You have become more than I could have dreamt, and now I see that same promise of eternal love in the eyes and smiles of your daughters. We are now the "Keepers of the Fire" forever lasting. You honor me, my "Butterfly."

I thank you my husband, Dr. Tatsuya Suda. When we met on a plane to Japan I recognized a kindness in your eyes like none I'd ever known. When I met your mother, Toshiko, I saw the same kindness in her face and I knew I was home. I watched you place your healing hands on my dying father and you soothed his pain. A few months later you stood selflessly by my side caring for my dying mother. You were beside me again giving me the strength and support following the tragic loss of Priscilla. Throughout the struggles, tragedies, and victories, you have been unwaveringly my partner and I love you.

Lastly, I thank my parents Dick and Charlotte Coolidge for allowing me to share the sacred space and to hold them and sing them over as they slipped through the fragile veil to the other side. They gave themselves to everyone but especially their children, Dick, Priscilla, Linda, and me, a solid foundation of family values and unconditional love to be passed on and on and on, foreverlasting.

Photographic Sources

Grateful acknowledgment is made to the following for permission to reproduce the illustrations found throughout the book:

About the Authors

RITA COOLIDGE is a two-time Grammy Award winner. She began her music career in Memphis before moving to Los Angeles, where she became one of the most popular backup singers in the business, recording with Leon Russell, Joe Cocker, Eric Clapton, Stephen Stills, and other artists. Signed to A&M Records as a solo artist in 1971, she released more than two dozen albums in the years that followed, including the multiplatinum *Anytime . . . Anywhere*, and continues to record and tour. She lives in Fallbrook, California.

MICHAEL WALKER is the bestselling author of *Laurel Canyon: The Inside Story of Rock-and-Roll's Legendary Neighborhood* and *What You Want Is in the Limo: On the Road with Led Zeppelin, Alice Cooper, and the Who in 1973, the Year the Sixties Died and the Modern Rock Star Was Born*. He has written about popular culture for the *New York Times* and is a contributing editor at the *Hollywood Reporter*. He lives in Los Angeles.